D1462089

Then to the Rock Let Me Fly

Then to the Rock Let Me Fly

LUTHER BOHANON AND JUDICIAL ACTIVISM

by Jace Weaver

FOREWORD BY ROBERT H. HENRY

UNIVERSITY OF OKLAHOMA PRESS : NORMAN AND LONDON

Published with the assistance of the National Endowment for the Humanities, a federal agency which supports the study of such fields as history, philosophy, literature, and language.

Text design by Bill Cason

R0123007437

SSCCA

Library of Congress Cataloging-in-Publication Data

Weaver, Jace, 1957— HOUSTON PUBLIC LIBRARY
Then to the rock let me fly : Luther Bohanon and judicial activism / by Jace Weaver ; foreword by Robert H. Henry.
    p. cm.
    Includes bibliographical references and index.
    ISBN 0–8061–2554–3 (alk. paper)
    1. Bohanon, Luther Lee, 1902– . 2. Judges—United States—Biography. 3. Civil rights—United States—History. I. Title.
KF373.B545W43   1993
347.73'2234—dc20
[B]
[347.307234]
[B]
                           93–2441
                             CIP

The paper in this book meets the guidelines for permanence and durability of the Committee on Production Guidelines for Book Longevity of the Council on Library Resources, Inc. ∞

Copyright © 1993 by the University of Oklahoma Press, Norman, Publishing Division of the University. All rights reserved. Manufactured in the U.S.A.

1   2   3   4   5   6   7   8   9   10

O Sometimes The Shadows Are Deep

O sometimes the shadows are deep,
And rough seems the path to the goal,
And sorrows, sometimes how they sweep
Like tempests down over the soul!

O then to the Rock let me fly,
To the Rock that is higher than I;
O then to the Rock let me fly,
To the Rock that is higher than I!

O sometimes how long seems the day,
And sometimes how weary my feet;
But toiling in life's dusty way,
The Rock's blessed shadow, how sweet!
[REFRAIN]

O near to the Rock let me keep
If blessings or sorrows prevail,
Or climbing the mountain way steep,
Or walking the shadowy vale.
[REFRAIN]

ERASTUS JOHNSON
1826–1909

Contents

Foreword, by Robert H. Henry   *page* xi
Preface   xv
  I. Invisible Tapestry   3
  II. A Life at Law   15
  III. The Judge   55
  IV. The School Board Case   71
  V. The Prison Case   117
  VI. The American Indian Land Case   138
VII. The Laetrile Case   146
Epilogue   157
Appendix. Published Opinions of
   Luther L. Bohanon   160
Notes   173
Bibliography   197
Index   207

Illustrations

Judge Luther Bohanon   *frontispiece*
The Bohanon family about 1912   22
Young Bohanon with wife, Marie, and friend
    Weldon Hall   39
Captain Luther Bohanon, U.S. Army Air Force,
    December 4, 1942   42

Foreword

by Robert H. Henry

IN a state noted for political mavericks, Luther Bohanon will certainly take a well-deserved place. At an age when he should have outlived his enemies, his name still evokes bitter controversy resulting from his constitutionally imposed advocacy for minorities and prisoners—indeed, the very people referred to in the scripture he quoted in a 1978 case, *Battle v. Anderson*:

For I was hungred, and ye gave me meat: I was thirsty, and ye gave me drink: I was a stranger, and ye took me in: Naked, and ye clothed me: I was sick and ye visited me: I was in prison, and ye came unto me.[1]

Judge Bohanon's Cincinnatus-like roots are not uncommon in Oklahoma's history. But he did not choose as his goal the governor's mansion, as did fellow agrarian William Henry ("Alfalfa Bill") Murray, nor did he choose the U.S. Senate, as did another plain-speaking farmer, Henry Bellmon. A very successful lawyer, Bohanon turned to politics as an interest, and his understanding of that sometimes dark art led to alliance and close friendship with Oklahoma's most dominant political power, the late Senator Robert S. Kerr.

Despite the improper opposition of the then-powerful American Bar Association, and what seemed to be the absolute enmity of Attorney General Robert Kennedy (as this book illustrates), Senator Kerr "explained" to a youthful president, who intuitively understood the powerful Sooner solon, that Luther Bohanon needed to be and would be a federal judge. So at age fifty-nine, after a brilliantly successful career, Bohanon began his real moment in the sun.

Few would have guessed the impact this solitary judge would have on his state and indeed on his nation. Influenced greatly by the two judges he most admired, Justices Earl Warren and William O. Douglas, Bohanon became a lightning rod for popular resistance to what is now considered mainstream legal thought. Eschewing the ignoble tradition of Southern judges who ignored the Civil War Amendments and ensuing cases, Bohanon became the rock to which the oppressed did indeed fly. Remembering the words of the God he so fervently worshiped, he reminded society in the most powerful prose of its responsibility to those imprisoned. Remembering his early affinity and work for Native Americans, Bohanon defended them in his decisions. Having a natural sympathy for the poor and ill, he aligned himself with them and against powerful bureaucracies in the Laetrile cases—which do not enjoy the same favored place in history that these other earlier decisions have now come to occupy. And yet Judge Bohanon is no judicial activist; his honor comes not from *creating* the law, but from courageously applying the law as he sees it to facts that he refuses to run from.

All of his life this feisty farmboy-turned-jurist has been a hard and seemingly tireless worker, both in the

physical work of the farm and in the extremely difficult task of reading and analyzing voluminous briefs
and books of the law. But throughout his career he
has reflected a simple Christian faith that values the
poor, the weak, the downtrodden, and the individual
in America. Ardent believer that he is, he does not
seek to impose his specific faith. Yet, throughout every
case he has written, one sees an absolute fidelity to
the Constitution and precedent as he sees them and,
for him, a not-inconsistent abiding religious faith that
is the hope of the powerless.

This book is a good part of the story of this unique,
courageous man. Once threatened, vilified in the papers, hung in effigy, "churched," assaulted, and dis-
dained, he has lived to see universities confer honorary
degrees on him and the legislature he once so vigor-
ously chided present him resolutions of commenda-
tion. At age ninety, still mounting a treadmill every
day for his personal constitutional, he continues to
climb the steps to the bench to dispense the justice he
derives from our nation's Constitution.

Basically, Luther Bohanon describes the very best in
the federal trial bench: a judge who hears the facts and
follows the law as he understands it with total disregard for external matters that should have no bearing
on the dispensation of justice. Unconcerned with pop-
ularity and fearless of the powerful forces who opposed
him, he has for over thirty years called cases as he saw
them. It is not essential to agree in every case with
Judge Bohanon; it is important to note, understand,
and admire his consistency and his worldview.

In this era of detailed diagnostic tests to determine
the political philosophy of federal judges, it is perhaps
unlikely that independent sorts like Luther Bohanon

will be easily appointed to the bench. However, as our founders realized, the independence of the judiciary is one of the most vital safeguards that the few have against the many. This book is a case study that stands for the vitality of our founders' view.

Preface

MALCOLM Muggeridge observed, "It often happens that the reason for doing something only emerges clearly after it has been done, conscious intent and all the various practicalities which go therewith being but the tip of an iceberg of unconscious intent."[1] Such must surely be the case with this book. The book began life as an idea for a collection of the many eloquent and important opinions authored by Judge Luther Bohanon. I felt that it was important to collect and preserve these in a single place, with brief introductions, so that both the student and the educated layperson could have easy access to them without the complicated hassle of legal research. The idea of a more formal, albeit brief and tentative, biography emerged only over time in conversations among Judge Bohanon, John Drayton of the University of Oklahoma Press, and me.

The purpose of this volume is to sketch the life and career of one trial court judge, Luther Bohanon, U.S. District Court judge for the Northern, Eastern, and Western districts of Oklahoma. Because in his more than thirty years on the bench Judge Bohanon has authored more than 180 published opinions, the decisions discussed herein must be, of necessity, only a small fraction of his total output. His opinions rate as some of the most eloquent and intelligent issued by a federal judge. His work deserves to be recorded and remembered.[2]

My great good fortune in writing this book is the degree of participation of Judge Bohanon himself in the process. This must be considered an authorized biography. As such it suffers from all the limitations of such a biography. I hope it also has some of the virtues. I have worked closely with Judge Bohanon for over two years to produce it, and he has become a friend in the process. It is not, however, a mere encomium, a record meant to stress noble achievements and character while excluding or glossing over questionable or derogatory events or traits. Neither the judge nor I are interested in having his story told in such a fashion. As a judge, Luther Bohanon has prided himself on allowing both sides to make a full and complete record and then letting the trier of fact decide regardless of which way the chips may fall. In reading this book, you are his trier of fact.

The book is, however, my own. The choices have been my own. Although I began and remain enormously positive about Judge Bohanon and his accomplishments, no man can remain (nor does he deserve to remain) entirely free from criticism. I have not always concurred with the choices he has made, and where this is true I have tried to make it known so that you, the reader, may decide for yourself. Judge Bohanon has at times disagreed vociferously with assessments I have made. In his cooperation, however, he has always been gracious enough to allow me the latitude to present an opposing point of view to his actions or those of others described herein. I sought the judge out and secured his participation. He has contributed countless hours of his time for interviews and has opened his private files and correspondence to me. The rest remains mine.

The title of the book is taken from an old Methodist camp meeting hymn, which has been taken by some to be an appropriate metaphor for the struggle of Oklahoma City African-Americans for civil rights. The rock of the title is obviously God, but as in the old black spirituals, the words of the song took on a second meaning. The rock was seen also as meaning the federal courts, to whom African-Americans repeatedly appealed for protection of their rights and which, at least for a time, vindicated those rights.

I am appreciative of those other than Judge Bohanon who gave me their time in interviews and cooperation, among them Clara Luper, Jack Greenberg, Julius Chambers, and Susan Heinze Ray, Judge Bohanon's longtime assistant. William A. Berry, justice of the Oklahoma Supreme Court from 1958 to 1978, helped me understand the *Selected Investments* case, which played an important role in Bohanon's career. Bert Barefoot, Jr., Bohanon's longtime law partner, shared his thoughts on the judge's career and character.

Much needed encouragement and advice were given during the completion of this project by many dear friends and relatives, chief among them my father, G. H. Weaver, Jr.; Susanna Shields of the firm of Proskauer, Rose, Goetz & Mendelsohn; Theodore Kovaleff, assistant dean of the Columbia Law School and a legal and economic historian;[3] John Drayton, editor-in-chief of the University of Oklahoma Press; George Robinson of the National Writers' Union; Jeff Zeitlin; and Roberto Voci, a fellow Oklahoma politician watcher and local photographer in Norman. I also owe a deep debt of gratitude to James Cone, my professor and mentor, who showed me in his book *Martin &*

Malcolm & America: A Dream or a Nightmare a new way to do theology—through narrative history; without him I would never have persevered to finish this book. In addition to these persons, several noted historians have been kind enough to review and comment on all or portions of my manuscript. These include Philip C. F. Bankwitz, distinguished professor emeritus of history at Trinity College; Martin S. Alexander, visiting professor of history at the U.S. Naval War College; and James M. Washington, civil rights historian and professor of history at Union Theological Seminary.[4] Their contributions have been an important part in the preparation and vetting of this work. And, of course, special thanks goes to Judge Luther L. Bohanon, without whose generous help and cooperation this book would not have been possible. I gratefully dedicate it to him and to the family and friends who stood by him during many dark and difficult times. I also dedicate it to my dear friend Duane Draper, lawyer and activist, who fought the good fight as long as he lived.

JACE GARRETT WEAVER

New York
February 4, 1992

Then to the Rock Let Me Fly

Chapter I

Invisible Tapestry

MOST opinions of U.S. district court judges are, to paraphrase Abraham Lincoln, neither little noted nor long remembered. Even when a case does capture our imaginations, usually it is only the Supreme Court opinion we remember. Who, after all, recalls who wrote the lower court opinions in *Brown* v. *Board of Education* or *Roe* v. *Wade* and what they said? Only a handful of appellate judges—Hand, Cardozo, Friendly—have achieved any degree of public recognition or lasting fame.

If, however, we neither note nor remember the words of district court judges, as with Lincoln's soldiers of Gettysburg, we cannot forget their deeds. The actions of federal trial courts form lasting threads in the invisible tapestry of social control that we call the law.

It is commonly stated that district court judges are to enforce the law, not make it. For example, in *Brown* v. *Board of Education*, at the trial court level, attorneys for the National Association for the Advancement of Colored People (NAACP) used existing case law to argue forcefully that segregation in and of itself, without more, violates rights guaranteed by the Fourteenth Amendment, a position never yet clearly taken by the Supreme Court. The district court, however, demurred from making such a finding, articulating instead the classic position of such courts:

This contention poses a question not free from difficulty. As a subordinate court in the federal judicial system, we seek to answer this constitutional question on the decisions of the Supreme Court when it has spoken on the subject and do not substitute our own views for the declared law by the Supreme Court. The difficult question as always is to analyze the decisions and seek to ascertain the trend as revealed by later cases.[1]

Such an articulation is, at best, an oversimplification. At worst it is manifestly incomplete. To show that trial judges change the law from time to time is easy. Such change is not only superficial as new conditions require adaptation of some old rule to fill some unexpected lacuna, but also fundamental as the ideals of our society evolve. Every case decided makes law by reinforcing the law's current state, by stretching its limits, or by altering its course in some way, be it major or minor. Precedents can be interpreted either narrowly or broadly.

The opinion of Judge J. Waties Waring in *Briggs* v. *Elliot*, one of the four school desegregation cases consolidated with *Brown*, provides a clear example of how district courts can view identical precedents and reach completely opposite conclusions. Unlike the trial court in *Brown*, Waring believed that *Plessy* v. *Ferguson*, the "separate but equal" opinion, was irrelevant and that the district court could rule in favor of the children without flouting the Supreme Court's stated views.[2] Every case presents what Harvard professor Archibald Cox terms "opportunities for choice."

In his book, *The Court and the Constitution*, Cox states that the law cannot be static if it is to meet the needs of society:

New situations continually arise. Some plainly fall outside any precedent. Others call for a choice between opposing precendents, which are somewhat analogous but also distinguishable. In such cases, conscious or inarticulate views of wise policy become decisive. Changes in conditions may rob legal concepts, rules, and even principles of their former meaning, so that old ideals and even traditional principles call for new forms of implementation. Better perception of the true meaning of basic ideals may call for new applications.

District court judges must follow precedent. This fundamental safeguard of our common-law system is called the principle of *stare decisis*. It ensures continuity and predictability in judicial decisions, and it means that persons can rely on case precedents in forming their actions. In one of the most damning statements made by Judge Robert Bork that ultimately led to his failure to be confirmed as a Supreme Court Justice, he said that he saw no particular need to be bound by precedent.

In the recent case of *Payne* v. *Tennessee* (S. Ct. June 27, 1991), Chief Justice William Rehnquist said that obeying precedent is "usually the wise policy" but that it was not an absolute, especially when the previous decision is "unworkable or badly reasoned." This provoked a blistering defense of *stare decisis* from Justice Thurgood Marshall in his final dissent on the Court. Marshall wrote, "Power, not reason, is the new currency of this court's decision making.... Cast aside today are those condemned to face society's ultimate penalty. Tomorrow's victims may be minorities, women or the indigent." He stated that "neither the law nor the facts ... underwent any change in the last four years [the elapsed time since the deciding of the precedent overruled by *Payne*]. Only the personnel of this Court did."

This debate is important because the principle has become a shuttlecock in the game of badminton which the debate over abortion has become. Pro-choice advocates contend that the right to an abortion has become "settled" and should not be rescinded. Antiabortion activists claim that the *Roe* v. *Wade* decision, which established the right, was incorrectly decided and should be overturned. In an interview, Judge Bohanon, a strong proponent of *stare decisis,* expressed his opinion that *Roe* should not be abandoned.[3]

Yet precedent should not, as already intimated, be followed slavishly. Judge Learned Hand spoke succinctly of the inherent dilemma in a judge's work when he wrote: "He must preserve his authority by cloaking himself in the majesty of an overshadowing past, but he must discover some composition with the dominant needs of his times."[4]

District courts are the lowest federal courts. Their job is to try cases in the first instance and to enforce the edicts of the Supreme Court.[5] As such, they are more directly involved with the people and have a more direct influence upon their day-to-day lives than the more august body. We may not remember that Walter Huxman handed down the first opinion in *Brown* v. *Board,* but we must never forget what brave district court judges such as Frank Johnson, Skelly Wright, and Luther Bohanon did to give teeth to the

Supreme Court's decree in that case. During much of the time it was the courts that spoke as the "national conscience" while legislatures and executives were silent.[6]

Walter August Huxman, circuit judge on the Tenth Circuit Court of Appeals, authored the *Brown* opinion for a three-judge panel composed of himself and District Judges Arthur J. Mellott and Delmas C. Hill. Three-judge district courts were a little-used feature of our judicial system which allowed a special three-judge panel to sit when the case asked for relief against federal, state, or municipal laws on the grounds that those laws were at odds with the U.S. Constitution. Appeals from three-judge courts are taken directly to the Supreme Court, bypassing the Circuit Courts of Appeals. The technique was perfected by NAACP lawyer Thurgood Marshall in *McLaurin* v. *Oklahoma State Board of Regents* in 1948 and later used in numerous civil rights cases, including *Brown* and *Dowell* v. *Oklahoma City School Board.*

Yet despite those efforts, as Derrick Bell, a professor at Harvard Law School and a former attorney with the NAACP, has stated, it was amazing "how many devices school boards and their lawyers worked out to convey a sense of compliance with *Brown,* while in fact the schools remained segregated. . . . Unravelling the seemingly neutral procedures contained in these plans to get at their segregation-maintaining intent proved a challenge for both civil rights lawyers and for many federal judges who were ostracized and abused for carrying out the *Brown* mandate."[7]

The decisions of Luther Bohanon deal with some of the most important issues of the past thirty years: integration and civil rights, sex discrimination, privacy and freedom of choice, penal reform, the rights of the

physically challenged, freedom of speech. His work
has been unquestionably important in the history of
Oklahoma and our nation. It helped make us a "freer,
more equal, and more humane society." At times the
strides may have seemed long, but that is only because
there was far to go.[8]

Yet, in a larger sense, Bohanon's career is merely representative of the federal judiciary at its best. Federal
courts, committed to the Constitution, have provided
the hard rock upon which we have stood in our strug-
gles for justice, equality and dignity and behind which
we have taken shelter when our most basic freedoms
have come under attack. Learned Hand, in writing
about Judge Benjamin Cardozo, stated that a judge's
"authority and immunity depend upon the assump-
tion that he speaks with the mouth of others: The mo-
mentum of his utterance must be greater than any
which his personal reputation and character can command, if it is to stand against the passionate resentments arising out of the interests he must frustrate."[9]

In his day, like any good jurist called upon to perform the tasks which have befallen him, Bohanon has
frustrated some powerful interests and, in the process,
has aroused some passionate resentments. It was not,
however, from his own authority that he acted. Rather,
he acted from the authority of the Constitution and
the U.S. government. As Judge Bohanon himself has
said, "The judiciary of this country is the bulwark of
this nation's security. Where people can go to court
and get justice, anarchy cannot exist."

By the time I met Luther Bohanon, he had "gone senior," having retired some years before. With his full
head of snowy white hair and his muttonchop side-
burns, he looked as though he belonged on the court
more in the time of Holmes, or even David Davis, than

in the late twentieth century. Surrounded in his chambers by paintings by Charles Russell and Frederick Remington, in the context of his workplace, one could get an idea of the kind of hard-edged justice he dispensed, not unlike, as McMichael and Coplin have observed, that of his distant predecessors who brought law to the American West.[10]

When I came to know him, in the early 1980s, his name was already anathema to a large segment of the Oklahoma population. He had believed that when the Supreme Court ordered desegregation of public schools with "all deliberate speed" it had meant with all deliberate speed, and when he found that pace more deliberate than speedy, he mandated a court-approved plan to accomplish it. He enforced the Civil Rights Act of 1964 and ended segregation in housing and the state militia. He had ruled in favor of equal treatment for women in the workplace.[11] When state penitentiaries were found to be denying inmates even the most fundamental human rights, he (despite his own protestations to the contrary) in effect took over the prison system and ran it from the bench. And when terminally ill cancer patients were prevented from importing the controversial drug laetrile, he enjoined the Food and Drug Administration, finding that the much debated constitutional right of privacy protected the patients' actions. For his efforts he was reviled, castigated in the press, and hanged in effigy. He had garbage dumped on his lawn and had his life threatened. I asked him why, despite all the opprobrium, he had taken those stands. He replied that he didn't know what else he could have done and still lived with his conscience. He had tried to live his life by a simple credo, one he had included in his biographical entry in Who's Who in America, "Do right and fear no man."[12]

Yet what impressed me most about Judge Bohanon was neither his physical appearance nor the respect I had for his record; what struck me was the way he spoke about the Constitution. He referred to it, certainly, as a rock but also as an organic entity, a living, breathing being. Others, too, have remarked on his "authoritative intimacy" with the law. A 1974 profile stated, "One is struck by how finely the U.S. Constitution is structured into Judge Bohanon's thinking. Phrases like 'due process' are used like guide posts to point the way to a finite justice. It is evident that Judge Bohanon knows of the sometimes awesome personal liberties guaranteed every citizen by the Constitution, and even more evident that he is aware of the absolute moral necessity of those liberties."[13]

President John Kennedy appointed Bohanon to the federal bench in 1961. The lifetime appointment, covering all three of Oklahoma's federal judicial districts, began on September 8, 1961.

In October 1961, Robert L. Dowell, through his father, Dr. A. L. Dowell, brought suit against the Oklahoma City School Board, seeking an end to continuing segregation in Oklahoma City public schools. Judge Bohanon, on the bench for only a month, was assigned to a three-judge panel to hear the case. When the special court was dissolved on July 10, 1962, as being without jurisdiction, the case, having been assigned originally to Bohanon, was handed back to him for further proceedings. After less than a year on the court, Luther Bohanon had the case of which he would later claim to be most proud and the case that would make him famous. Thirty years later, he has entered only recently what may be his final opinion in *Dowell* v. *Board of Education of Oklahoma City*. In affirming

one of his orders in *Dowell* in 1970, the U.S. Court of
Appeals for the Tenth Circuit said that he "had faced
many unusually difficult situations in his enforcement
of the mandates of the Supreme Court and . . . acted in
an effective and skillful way. The record in this and the
related cases demonstrates that little or no action
would have been taken by the Board of Education
without his 'encouragement.' "[14]

In his years on the court, Judge Bohanon would decide cases covering the rights of minorities, women,
children, the terminally ill, the physically challenged,
and prison inmates. A man of tremendous personal up-
rightness, he would say, "A lawyer must possess and
demonstrate integrity and fidelity. He should always
treat his client's business as if he knew his client was
in the ceiling of his office, looking down seeing and
hearing everything his attorney does and has to say
about his client's business."[15] For thirty years, he has
treated those who have come before him seeking protection of their civil rights and civil liberties as though
they were his clients.

A devout Christian, a Methodist, Judge Bohanon
punctuated his third opinion in *Battle* v. *Anderson*,
the prison case discussed herein, with a quotation
from the scriptures: *"For I was hungred, and ye gave
me meat: I was thirsty, and ye gave me drink: I was a
stranger, and ye took me in: Naked, and ye clothed
me: I was sick, and ye visited me: I was in prison, and
ye came unto me."*[16]

Retired for more than four years at the time, perhaps
he felt that *Battle III* was his valediction. It was an en-
capsulation of his judicial philosophy and would have
been a fitting farewell, but he continues to sit and decide cases ten years later. Like another Oklahoman,

Steinbeck's Tom Joad, Luther Bohanon continues to be there when human rights and dignity are at stake.

The thirty years in which Judge Bohanon has served in the federal judiciary have witnessed a tremendous constitutional upheaval as aggrieved minorities and other persons secured their rights with the aid of the federal courts. This upheaval, in turn, created a vocal opposition among conservative elements of our society who decried federal judges for wanting to substitute their views for those of elected legislatures. The backlash created by this so-called judicial activism led to a variety of proposals to trim the power of the courts. Jesse Helms obtained substantial support for a proposal to strip federal courts of the power to hear cases involving school prayer or abortion. Senator David Boren, who as governor of Oklahoma had opposed Bohanon in the prison case, proposed a constitutional amendment to end life tenure for federal judges. Some have even proposed electing federal judges in the manner of state judges.[17]

Others, like Pulitzer Prize–winning columnist Murray Kempton, take issue with this analysis of "judicial activism," pointing out its inherent flaw. He has written,

Complying with the will of the state is as activist an endeavor as resisting it. And the function of judicial review, in the most critical instance is, if not to resist, at least to check the majoritarian will as expressed in the state.... *Brown v. Board of Education* was in its essence an affirmation of what it is permissible for the state to do to the citizen. Segregation was, after all, a legal entity established by legislatures and administered by governors. It was the rule of a minority by a majority; and the Supreme Court that overturned it was not legislating but telling the legislatures what the Constitution would not let them do.[18]

Kempton and those who view the judiciary as he does see the current system as the bulwark of our security. Senator Sam Ervin stated, "To my mind an independent judiciary is perhaps the most essential characteristic of a free society."[19]

In order to ensure the independence of that judiciary, the framers of our Constitution provided in Article III for life tenure and a guarantee against reduction in compensation. When James Madison proposed the first ten amendments to that Constitution, the Bill of Rights, he said that "independent tribunals of Justice will consider themselves in a peculiar manner the guardian of those rights."[20] Chancellor James Kent, the father of American jurisprudence, stated that the provisions for life tenure and support for judges were "admirably fitted to produce the free exercise of judgment in the discharge of their trust."

Kent could have been writing about any of several of Bohanon's cases when he wrote of an independent judiciary:

In monarchial governments, the independence of the judiciary is essential to guard the rights of the subject from the injustice of the crown; but in republics it is equally salutary, in protecting the constitution and laws, from the encroachments and the tyranny of faction. Laws, however wholesome or necessary, are frequently the object of temporary aversion, and sometimes popular resistance. It is requisite that the courts of justice should be able, at all times, to present a determined countenance against all licentious acts; and to give them a firmness to do it, the judges ought to be confident of the security of their stations. Nor is an independent judiciary less useful as a check upon the legislative power, which is sometimes disposed, from the force of passion, or the temptations of interest, to make a sacrifice of constitutional rights; and it is a wise and necessary princi-

ple of our government . . . that legislative acts are subject to
the severe scrutiny and impartial interpretation of the courts
of justice, who are bound to regard the constitution as the
paramount law, and the highest evidence of the will of
the people.[21]

Thomas Jefferson, later to clash with Chief Justice
John Marshall on the question of presidential power,
believed that "the laws of the land, administered by
upright judges," would protect the people from any unconstitutional exercise of power.[22]

Harvard's Professor Cox has written of the necessary
independence of the judiciary: "The loss of independence would endanger the basic values of constitu-
tionalism. The very purpose of written constitutions
containing Bills of Rights and guaranteeing judicial independence was to put some rights beyond the reach of
government policy, even beyond the power of a majority of the people. Judicial interpretation gives better
protection than the political branches to unpopular individuals and minorities shut out of, or inadequately
represented in, the political process."[23] Judge Bohanon
would agree with him: "Where people can go to court
and get justice, anarchy cannot exist."

Luther Bohanon is only one federal judge. Most people outside of Oklahoma have never heard of him.
Increasing numbers of Oklahomans, in fact, do not
remember him. Yet he and his colleagues on the bench
have helped shape our understanding of ourselves.
They have told us who we are by reminding us of
what we might be.[24] That alone makes them worth
remembering.

Chapter II

A Life at Law

ARCHIBALD Cox observed that while the opinions of the nation's courts can sometimes be "the voice of the spirit reminding us of our better selves," the roots of such decisions must lie already in the hearts of the people. He wrote, "The aspirations voiced by the Court must be those that the community is willing not only to avow but in the end to live by. The legitimacy of the great creative decisions of the past flowed in large measure from the accuracy of the Court's perception of this kind of common will and from the Court's ability, by expressing the perception, to strike a responsive chord equivalent to the consent of the governed." Professor William Young of Columbia Law School voiced a similar opinion when he said that we, as a society, must be very careful about how we administer the law or we will lose all support for its use.[1]

Perhaps in those statements Professors Cox and Young provided a clue to why Judge Bohanon, often despite tremendous public opposition at the time, was able ultimately to succeed in enforcing his decisions and why now, late in his career, he is held in such high regard. Whether we were always willing to acknowl-

edge it or not, in his decision he spoke for "the better angels of our nature." He sought to protect those
broad-based freedoms which we claim fundamental to
our self-identification as a nation. Arthur Laurents describes Hubbell Gardner, the golden-boy hero of his
novel *The Way We Were*, by saying, "In a way he was
like the country he lived in—everything came too easily." While nothing in the life of Luther Bohanon has
come easily, in a very different way he personifies the
country in which he was born. His life can be seen as a
model of the so-called American Dream, embodying
the hopes and values that we all absorbed from gram-
mar school civics texts.

Bohanon's paternal grandparents, Lewis and Mary
Bohannon were Norwegian-Americans from Lebanon,
Missouri, in the southern portion of that state, deep
in the Ozarks. It was there that his father, William Joseph Bohannon, was born in 1860. Wanting to simplify
the spelling of the family name, William would later
change it to Bohanon. Judge Bohanon, in fact, has been
able to trace the family name back to Norway, where
originally it was Boha.[2]

The year following William's birth, the Civil War
erupted. Missouri was a border state, and the citizens
joined the armies of both sides. Lewis Bohannon supported the Confederacy and was killed in battle. When
Union troops reoccupied the region, Mary Bohannon
and her son fled with other Southern sympathizers to
Texas.

In 1887, William Bohanon married Artelia Hickman,
known most often simply as Telia. During the next
thirteen years, William and Telia moved a great deal
from place to place as William farmed and did odd jobs.
They raised six children, and although they were never

what could be called prosperous, they eked out a modest existence.[3]

Luther Lee Bohanon was born on August 9, 1902, in Fort Smith, Arkansas, where William operated the Silver Dollar Saloon and the nearby livery stable. Less than a year after Luther's birth, Telia died. Faced with the prospect of raising seven children, ranging in age from fifteen years to eight months, alone, William Bohanon married Lucy Alice Cain Cox on September 9, 1903. It was Lucy Bohanon who would raise Luther and whom he would always call Mama.

In June 1898, Congress passed the Curtis Act, which declared all agricultural leases held by non-Indians in Indian Territory void as of January 1, 1900. No longer able to maintain his farm in the Choctaw Nation, the elder Bohanon abandoned farming and moved to Arkansas. When the financial panic of 1905 forced him to sell the saloon and livery, he again looked toward Oklahoma. With the movement to unite the Twin Territories—Oklahoma and Indian—well underway, he recognized that statehood would result in the lifting of all restrictions on land tenure. Returning to Stigler in the Choctaw Nation, he took a job as a salesman for the Dobbins and Lance Hardware and Farm Implement Company.

Oklahoma joined the Union on November 16, 1907. Although he was only five years old at the time, Luther Bohanon always remembered the jubilation and excitement of the people on that day when they acceded to full membership in the United States. At the height of the celebration, the livery stable horses, released by some overzealous celebrant, stampeded down the street in front of the Bohanon household. Young Luther stood and stared as the terrified animals ran head-

long down the road and on out into the open prairie.
His most vivid memory, discussed in his unpublished
autobiographical manuscript, was of one horse so excited that it ran straight into a tree stump and fell over
dead directly in front of him.

With statehood, all federal restrictions on landown-
ership in Oklahoma lapsed. Almost immediately, William Bohanon traded the family piano for a wagon
and a team of mules, loaded up his family and furni-
ture, and moved to Blaine Bottom. Formally known as
Panola, the Choctaw word for cotton, Blaine Bottom
was about seven miles northeast of Keota, just across
the Arkansas River from Vian. There Bohanon, his
wife, and now ten children lived in a two-room log
cabin built on the side of the hill.

In Blaine Bottom, Luther began attending school in
a one-room schoolhouse where a single teacher taught
all grades the three *R*s. Perhaps significantly for his
later civil rights decisions, Luther and his brothers
and sisters were the only whites attending an otherwise all-Indian school. In fact, throughout this period,
wherever the Bohanon family moved, the children
were a decided minority of whites among Indians in
the schools they attended.

While the family was not exactly destitute, there
was little extra money, and with twelve mouths to
feed, Luther and his brothers were expected to help put
food on the table when they were not in school. Like
most of their neighbors, they supplemented their diet
with wild game, especially in the winter. The cane-
brakes that covered much of the area around the Arkansas River were filled with larger eight- to ten-
pound swamp rabbits, and Luther would often take the
family dog, Roller, into the swamps in search of food.
As he would later write: "I soon perfected the tech-

nique of walking noisily through the cane with the dog
until we flushed a rabbit. After the dog cornered the
animal in a hollow log or hollow tree, I would take a 4
to 5-foot length of limb, with a fork on the small end,
run it into the hiding place and twist it into the rabbit's fur. When the rabbit was hooked I slowly would
pull it out and take it home. We proudly called ourselves 'rabbit twisters.' "[4]

Lucy Bohanon was a great influence on Luther during these formative years. She had been raised in a
strict Mississippi Baptist home and insisted that her
new family respect her beliefs. Card playing, drinking, and dancing of any kind, including square dancing, were absolutely forbidden. All transgressions were
swiftly punished with a green switch from her peach
tree.

Sunday was an important day in the Bohanon household. As often as possible, Lucy would take the children to the nearest Baptist church to receive proper
religious instruction. When this was not possible she
"continually imparted her faith to her children." At
her urging, Luther was baptized into the church at
Beaver Creek. Although he would later switch to the
Methodist church, throughout his life and career, Luther Bohanon would always take seriously the commitment he made that day to, as he put it, "accept
Christ as my saviour" and all that such a commitment
entailed.[5]

Sunday was an important day in another respect. It
was the social center of the week, celebrated with an
old-fashioned Sunday dinner. Years later, Judge Bohanon would remember:

My stepmother would choose 4 or 5 chickens from the flock
of 200 to 300 and fry them for Sunday dinner. She took great

care to ensure that everyone had two or three pieces of chicken. Rounding out the meal was mashed potatoes, gravy, homemade cornbread, green beans, sweet potatoes, and sometimes turnips. During the summer months she also would serve radishes, greens, onions, and lettuce from her garden and we always had a plentiful supply of sweet or butter milk and churned butter. For dessert mama always baked a five-layer cake as well as a blackberry, apple, or dewberry pie, or peach pudding. Other times we were treated to homemade ice cream.[6]

The other great influence on Luther during this period was, of course, his father. He remembers him as a good, honest man, a hard worker and a strict disciplinarian. William taught his family to be, like other frontier families, self-sufficient and self-reliant. Family was crucial to survival, and fidelity to it was a primary responsibility. Both loyalty to family and friends and the pioneer's sense of self-reliance would serve Judge Bohanon well during his years on the bench when he incurred ridicule and attack for his controversial decisions.

Just to the north of the family homesite, which was three miles northeast of Kinta, was a large bluff, and below the bluff to the north was Fish Creek, where the family would swim during the summer. Like most small children, Luther had a dread of having his head underwater. Because he was unsure of his swimming ability, he spent most of the time dog-paddling near the water's edge. William, who believed that everyone should be a strong swimmer, patiently waited for the boy to become proficient, but when Luther persisted in paddling near the shore, William lured the boy onto a log across the swimming hole and then threw him in. When Luther popped to the surface he was swimming as well as any of his older brothers. The lesson was not lost on the young boy. Never again would Luther Bohanon hesitate, out of fear, to do anything.

In November 1908, William Bohanon moved his family again, and their fortunes began to turn upward. He received a contract from the Oklahoma Pipe Line Company to haul pipe about ten miles across the San Bois Mountains in Haskell and Latimer counties to help complete the pipeline which ran from Glennpool, near Tulsa, to Beaumont, Texas. He provided four log wagons each pulled by two teams of mules. For this he made eighty dollars a day, which provided him with sufficient capital to expand his farming operations. He concluded an arrangement with George Scott, his landlord and the son-in-law of Choctaw Governor Green McCurtain, whereby Bohanon would clear 480 acres of bottomland along San Bois Creek in exchange for title to 320 acres and a five-year lease on the remaining section. Once cleared of trees and brush, the land would produce forty to sixty bushels of corn or one-half bale of cotton per acre. Corn would go to feed the livestock and fatten the hogs, and cotton would be the cash crop. Cotton bales weighed five hundred pounds, and baled cotton sold for about fifteen cents a pound.[7] The goal was to raise thirty bales a year. Bohanon practiced crop rotation and introduced mechanization to the farm.

For the next few years, the family routine varied little. The boys would go to school until March, when they would leave to help with the plowing. They would return to school each November after the harvest.

In the spring of 1918, a seemingly small event occurred which would change Luther Bohanon's life forever. He walked Helen Smith, a classmate, home from school, and upon reaching her house, the girl's father

The Bohanon family about 1912. Back row: Agnes Bohanon Lewis, Lucy Cain Cox Bohanon, William Bohanon. Front row: Thornton Cox, Luther, Cecil, Wayman Cox, Herbert, Eileen, Joe.

invited him in. During the course of their conversation, Helen's father, who worked for the Oklahoma Pipe Line Company, suggested that Luther learn telegraphy and told him that, once he mastered the art, he would give him a job as a lineman. The idea appealed to the boy. He quickly acquired a Morse Code handbook and telegraph key, and six weeks later he could proficiently send and receive coded messages.

When Luther graduated from the eighth grade later that spring, he took a job as a pipeline walker, tracing a 100-mile circuit every week for the munificent salary

of $125 a month. He decided to continue his school-
ing. "If I could learn Morse Code in six weeks and im-
prove my earning capacity from $1.00 per day to $125
per month," Bohanon wrote, "what could I earn if I
went through college?" In his autobiography, Bohanon
writes, "As a farm boy, one works from sunup to sun-
down, and from the time I was eight years old I would
follow the walking plow, hoeing and thinning cotton
and corn. A decade of farm work made me dream of a
better life. In doing so, I realized that education was
the only out."[8] Thus began what can perhaps best be
described as an obsession with learning and school, an
obsession that would soon bring the young man into
conflict with his family.

A short time later, an altercation with Lucy Bohanon over Luther's failure to pay room and board
led William to tell his son that it was time for him "to
get my duds and get out."[9] Eager to be moving on, the
young Bohanon was not troubled by the instruction.
That night, he walked into Kinta and purchased a card-
board suitcase. The next day, he packed his worn-out
clothes and quit his job with the pipeline company.
The following day, at sixteen years old, he caught the
train to Muskogee, Oklahoma.

In Muskogee, Luther took up residence at the local
YMCA and found a job at the Sawolka Cafeteria,
owned and operated by Alice Robertson, who in the
Harding landslide of 1920 would become Oklahoma's
first and only female member of Congress and the only
Republican to that date from the Second Congressional District. He bussed tables during lunch from
11:30 to 1:30 and again from 5:30 to 7:30, attending
Central High School and studying during the rest of
the day. From 8:00 to 10:00 at night he registered
guests at the Y in exchange for his room. He also took

a job collecting overdue bills for the Empire Electric Company. He kept the three jobs for the four years he attended high school and was able to save three hundred dollars, which he invested in oil properties and promptly lost.

While in high school, the idea of becoming a lawyer began to take form in Luther's mind. Those who would become his professional idols emerged. He has stated that during the period he "read everything I could get my hands on about Daniel Webster and Lincoln."[10]

An incident during that time serves to illustrate Bohanon's commitment to education. In his autobiography he writes, "At the end of my first year of high school, having made passing grades in all subjects, I felt very good. Unfortunately in the summer of 1919 the prospect of me continuing my education received a blow." The "blow" came as his older brother Cecil was discharged from the army and stopped to visit Luther on his way home to Kinta.

When Luther told his brother of his educational plans, Cecil replied that he had always wanted to pursue his schooling as well. Excited that his brother shared his ambition, Luther said that he thought it was a fine idea, but he cautioned Cecil to register, as Luther had done, as a resident of Muskogee instead of Kinta, because if he were to enroll as a resident of Haskell County he would have to pay tuition of seventy-five dollars a semester.

Bohanon thought his brother understood, especially after he had explained to Cecil that if he listed a Haskell County residence, then Luther would have to pay the same tuition, which he could not afford. Nevertheless, when Cecil completed his enrollment papers, he listed Kinta in Haskell County as his home address. When school officials informed him that he would be required to pay the tuition, he replied, "Why, my brother, Luther, is going to school and he doesn't have to pay." Rather than pay the fee, Cecil refused to register and told Luther what had happened. The younger Bohanon was "frantic" that he would have to give up his dream of an education and "decided to do everything possible to remain in school."

For several days Luther dodged repeated requests to report to the principal's office. On one occasion, Coreen Battles, the secretary to the principal, came and removed him from class, stating that he must come with her to see the principal. The boy asked for permission to go to the bathroom first. While he was in the boy's restroom, the bell rang. While the halls were filled with students, he mingled with the crowd and escaped from the building.

Finally, realizing that he could not evade the authorities indefinitely, Bohanon reported to school assistant principal C. K. Reiff. Reiff listened to the boy's story and recognized his fervent desire to get a formal education. Moved, he agreed to let the student continue at Muskogee High School without payment of the registration fee. Bohanon has stated that he has remained grateful to Reiff throughout his life. He graduated in 1922.

The story shows the lengths to which the young Bohanon was willing to go to accomplish his goal of an education. Perhaps more significant, however, was his reaction to his family as a result of the incident. So obsessed was he with completing his schooling that he came to believe that his brother's motive was to "prevent me from continuing my education." In his conversations with Reiff, he said as much. This was more than sibling jealousy. Although he has subsequently denied it, at the time he probably could not help but

discern, rightly or wrongly, the hand of William Bohanon in the affair. The father had no desire to see his son
complete school. Rather, he wanted the boy to return
home and become a farmer and saw education as an in-
hibitor to these plans.

During the summer of 1919, Dr. J. E. Shelton, a local
dentist, persuaded Luther to join the Oklahoma National Guard, explaining that he would be sent to Fort
Sill for training that August and then would earn extra
money by attending weekly drills. When his employer,
Alice Robertson, stated that she would hold his job
while he was away at basic training, Bohanon decided
to enlist.

Although Bohanon was not yet eighteen, the recruit-
ing officer decided to waive the age limit and allowed
him to join. On a hot August day, Bohanon boarded the
train for Fort Sill with other members of his unit. It
was his first overnight train ride, and although there
was much drinking, singing, and dice playing, Bohanon, remembering his strict upbringing, refrained from
participating.

The group arrived in Fort Sill at 4:00 P.M. the following day and was immediately marched the five miles
to camp in full pack with their 1903 Springfield rifles
slung over their shoulders.

The next day reveille was at 6:00 A.M. The latrine in
the tent city was not in full operation, so many of the
men, including Bohanon, had to go to a nearby stream.
While there, Bohanon reflected on a day ahead filled
with drilling with the heavy Springfield rifle. In order
to get out of drill, he decided to walk into the nearby
town of Lawton. There he went to every movie he
could find. Upon his return to camp some twelve
hours later, he was taken to the company commander,
Captain Barnes, and assigned to kitchen police. To his

surprise, he found that duty preferable to drill and soon became the company cook, rising to the rank of sergeant before the end of training that summer.

After graduating from high school in Muskogee in 1922, Bohanon, at his father's request, returned to work on the family farm, now located near Hominy, Oklahoma. While at home that summer, Luther explained to his father his plans to attend the University of Oklahoma in the fall. The elder Bohanon objected, saying once again that he wanted Luther to remain on the farm. Finally, although he had trouble understanding how much it meant to Luther to go to college, William agreed in August to drive his son to Hominy, where he could catch the train to Oklahoma City. There the younger Bohanon planned to work until the school semester began.

When the day arrived, Luther hitched the team to their old Webber wagon, packed his bags with all his worldly possessions, and rode into town with his father. During the trip the boy asked his father to advance him one hundred dollars for the work he had done during the summer, explaining that he needed the money to pay for college. Although he had not broached the subject until they were almost to town, Luther was shocked when his father replied that he did not have that much cash and instead offered him ten dollars.

By the time the pair arrived at the wagonyard, the son was so angry that he simply walked away without a word, no doubt convinced that this was merely yet another attempt by his father to thwart his dream of an education. Years later, Judge Bohanon would say, "Fortunately we had arrived several hours before the train time, and by the time the train was scheduled to depart for Oklahoma City I had cooled my temper and decided that $10.00 was better than none at all. I searched until I found my father, who had stayed in Hominy to see me off, and told him that I had changed my mind and would take the $10.00."[11] The father replied simply, "Good," and together they walked to the railroad station, where he bought Luther a ticket to Oklahoma City and handed him the ten dollars. Luther Bohanon left for college.

Upon arriving in Oklahoma City, Bohanon went directly to the local YMCA and checked in. With only ten dollars in his pocket, he knew that he had to find a job quickly unless the manager of the Y would extend him credit. Touring the facility, he found a cot on the roof. The weather was still warm, so he checked out and secretly moved onto the rooftop. He slept on the cot and sneaked down to the top floor every morning to shower and shave unnoticed by the manager or the other residents.[12]

Bohanon contacted one of the former customers of Alice Robertson's Sawolka Cafeteria, William Emerson, a vice-president at Oklahoma Gas and Electric Company (OG&E), to inquire about the possibility of employment. Although Emerson was sympathetic to Bohanon's situation, he explained that there were no positions open. Bohanon responded that he would look around and find something that needed doing at OG&E, and if they wanted to pay him, they could; otherwise, he would work for free. Impressed by the young man's willingness to work without pay, Emerson told him, "If you feel like that, I'll find something for you to do," and he put him to work typing metal address plates for customer bills. Between August and September, Bohanon earned about eighty dollars, which he used to pay his tuition at the university.

In the fall of 1922, Bohanon was twenty years old

and had decided to become an attorney, having ruled
out the only other two professions he had considered,
architect and physician, as taking too long to accomplish. Unfortunately, when he tried to enroll in the
University of Oklahoma School of Law, he was told
that any entering freshman in the law school who was
under twenty-one was required to have completed
thirty hours of undergraduate work before matricu-
lation. This requirement could be completed in two
semesters. Much to his chagrin, however, Bohanon
learned that, beginning in 1923, the requirement
would be increased to sixty hours. Not wanting to
spend (he would say "waste") two years in college, he
sought to avoid the delay by writing that he was
twenty-one on his application.[13]

At that time, Julien Monnet, the dean of the law
school, required that all incoming freshmen be interviewed personally by him. When Bohanon was called
into Dean Monnet's office for his interview, Monnet
invited him to be seated and, after examining his application, asked, "Are you sure you are twenty-one years
of age?" Without hesitating, Bohanon replied that he
was. Unconvinced, Monnet commented on the appli-
cant's youthful appearance and then asked if he had
served in the Great War. Bohanon said that he had not.
Pointing out that if he were twenty-one he would have
been old enough for military service, Monnet continued, "Were you disabled or something?" Realizing that
he had been caught in his deception, Bohanon con-
fessed, "Dean, I wasn't honest with you, but I have to
work my way through school, and I don't see how I can
spend more than three years completing my legal education. Five years is just too long."[14]

Dean Monnet patiently explained that he had just
succeeded in qualifying the School of Law for admis-

sion to the American College of Law Association and that the rules of that organization required the completion of sixty hours of academic work prior to admission, beginning in September of 1922. In addition, the dean pointed out, that requirement would soon be increased to completion of a bachelor's degree. When the young Bohanon protested that he was not interested in an undergraduate degree but only wanted to practice law, Monnet stated that he was not thinking the situation through clearly. If he did, Monnet insisted, he would see that the education he would receive would prove a valuable asset in the practice of law. Monnet suggested that he get a job as a clerk in a local law office, where he could gain practical experience while completing the required undergraduate work before entering law school.

Bohanon took the dean's advice. For two years at the university he studied English, history, geology, and constitutional law. Upon completion of the required sixty hours of work, he was admitted to law school in the fall of 1924. As a result of his advice and the interest he took in Bohanon throughout his education, Monnet became a "special friend" of the future judge.[15]

In law school, Monnet taught his students that it was their personal duty to ensure that the Constitution never be set aside. "Stand by the Constitution" was a favorite phrase of his. He declared that the lawyers he trained must always do so regardless of the costs. He emphasized Article VI of the Constitution, which stated that the Constitution was "the supreme Law of the Land; and Judges in every State shall be bound thereby, anything in the Constitution or Laws of any State notwithstanding."[16]

While such precepts may sound simplistic today, it must be understood that at the time, they stood at the center of a great controversy among lawyers and legal scholars. Some, like Dean Monnet, expressed a faith that the law has a separate existence from human public affairs, "not merely because it applies to all men equally but because it binds the judges as well as the judged, not just today but yesterday and tomorrow." Others poked fun at those who believed in "the law up there, . . . a brooding omnipresence in the sky."[17]

Chief among the members of the latter group was Oliver Wendell Holmes, justice of the U.S. Supreme Court, who had declared that eventually the entire law would be rewritten, "discarding tradition and vague sentiment. Sociology and physiology would be its basis, for the foundations of the law ought to be scientifically designed to attain the goal of the social organism: survival. The law would be remade 'once and for all, like a yacht, on the lines of least resistance.' " For these "legal realist" scholars, the law becomes a mere tool of social policy: "the social good, not adherence to law, becomes the judge's obligation." Chief Justice Charles Evans Hughes would express the height of legal realism when he declared that the law meant whatever judges said it meant at any given time. Holmes himself expressed an opinion not unlike that of Hughes when he voiced his belief that the law was whatever courts would enforce. "The only question for lawyers," he wrote, "is how will the judges act."[18]

Such opinions were repugnant to Dean Monnet, and his teachings had great influence on jurisprudence in Oklahoma. Although legal realism, as embodied by Holmes, gradually became dominant in the courts, in law schools, and in the legal profession in general, this was not so in Oklahoma, where Monnet trained generations of attorneys. In one class alone, Bohanon's graduating class of 1927, Dean Monnet had trained a chief justice of the Oklahoma Supreme Court, two U.S. district court judges, two presiding judges of the Oklahoma Court of Criminal Appeals, a special justice of the Oklahoma Supreme Court, a judge of the state's Industrial Court, a judge of the Court of Tax Review, five state district judges, and six county judges. In addition, the class produced two state senators, three members of the state House of Representatives, and five members of various boards and commissions.[19]

Monnet's students saw his principles at work in his own life. His views brought opposition not only from other legal scholars but from legislators as well. His fidelity to the Constitution and his belief that it barred segregation and discrimination between the races brought him into frequent conflict with Oklahoma lawmakers in the early Jim Crow years of statehood. He was among the first to label Oklahoma's Grandfather Clause unconstitutional. Monnet was never uncertain of his opinions concerning constitutional law. Years later, in dedicating a statue to his old mentor, Judge Bohanon explained that "there can be no more fitting memorial to Dean Julien Charles Monnet than to remember that he instilled in us and into education of lawyers in Oklahoma, the respect, the awe, and love, with which we must approach, protect and uphold the Constitution and its principles."[20]

Monnet taught Oklahoma's future officers of the court that while the "words of the Bible guide us to things eternal, as Americans we are ... governed by the Constitution of the United States." The Constitution, he declared, was, with the exception of the Bible, the greatest document ever conceived by humanity.[21]

Such teachings had a profound effect upon Luther

Bohanon. Coming, as he did, from a strict religious background, he simply transferred a portion of his allegiance to a second absolute, the Constitution of the United States. In this regard, although their legal philosophies are in some ways diametrically opposed, it is interesting to note that Holmes and Bohanon had similar conservative religious upbringings. In his biography of Holmes, attorney Sheldon Novick points out that Holmes as a child attended church every Sunday in "half-Puritan Boston," followed by the ritual of Sunday dinner. After Sunday dinner, Holmes was not permitted to go outside or play. His life was "constrained" by the family's religious observation.[22]

When a monument was erected to Dean Monnet in front of the School of Law, the sponsoring committee, of which Bohanon was a part, would see added to its base a quote that read: "God's laws are immutable, the human family is always striving to understand these great laws of life. Let us who have become the administrators of man's law keep changing and blending these laws until they are one with the laws of our beloved Creator."[23]

During his five years of higher education, Bohanon worked at a variety of jobs, from manager of the Sigma Nu fraternity to bank bookkeeper to summer park ranger at Yellowstone National Park. Still, when it came time to graduate from law school, he had over one hundred dollars in outstanding bills with local merchants. This was particularly problematic because the University of Oklahoma required that before graduation each student pay in full all indebtedness owed to Norman shopkeepers. With no other way to pay his debts, Bohanon persuaded Ben Owen, the university's football coach and a personal friend, to cosign a note with him. On June 17, 1927, Luther Bohanon graduated from the University of Oklahoma School of Law. "Although I had fulfilled my dream of an education, I was broke," he would later remember.

Bohanon still lacked the fifteen dollars for the bar entrance fee which he would have to pay to the clerk of the Oklahoma Supreme Court before he could be sworn in as a lawyer. On the day he was scheduled to be called before the Oklahoma Supreme Court to take the oath on application of Dean Monnet,[24] he visited T. J. Woodmansee, a fraternity brother and a teller at the First National Bank of Oklahoma City. Going to Woodmansee's window at the bank, Bohanon handed him a counter check for twenty-five dollars payable to him. Bohanon explained that he needed the money to be sworn in as an attorney. Although Woodmansee knew that his friend did not have an account at the bank, he agreed to loan him the money personally, taking the check as an IOU. Thus Luther Bohanon finished law school the way he had entered it, with an uncertain future and ten dollars of borrowed money in his pocket.

Although he had been offered a position with an established law office in Oklahoma City, Bohanon was determined to build his own legal practice, and so he left for Seminole, Oklahoma. Seminole County and the surrounding area were the site of phenomenal oil and gas production, with five of the largest oil fields ever located in the United States being discovered there in rapid succession. Seminole itself was the epitome of the oil boomtown, flooded with oilmen, scouts, and promoters of every stripe. Men slept anywhere they could—in tents, on pool tables, in movie theatres, in chicken coops and coal sheds.

Although he knew no one in Seminole when he stepped off the train, Bohanon was determined to build a practice there. Within a short time he met a lawyer named Wilkinson who had given up the practice of law for the more lucrative job of real estate agent and lease hound. In exchange for office space, a telephone, and some secretarial help from Wilkinson's wife, Bohanon agreed to handle his paperwork.

While this enabled Bohanon to pay his bills, he did not consider the arrangement to be a permanent one, and in August he went to see another fraternity brother, Oral Busby, state district judge for Pontotoc County. Because the courts in Seminole County had been overwhelmed by the huge influx of men lured by the oil boom, Busby was also doing additional judicial work there, sitting in Wewoka, the county seat. When he learned that Bohanon was hoping to establish his own practice in Seminole, Busby asked if he would be interested in a position with the county attorney's office. Bohanon quickly said yes, and Judge Busby telephoned Homer Bishop, the Seminole County attorney, saying that he thought Bohanon would make an excellent assistant county attorney. After interviewing the young man, Bishop hired him. The job paid $125 a month, the same amount Bohanon had earned as a pipeline walker almost ten years earlier.

For the next two weeks, Bohanon watched Bishop in action in Wewoka, and in that short time he learned the basics of criminal procedure, how to draw criminal complaints, how to issue arrest warrants, and, most important, how to handle the sheriff's office. During that time his main task was to go to the county jail with his files on all prisoners who had not yet been interviewed and to present the county attorney's case so convincingly that the suspect would plead guilty and thus save the county the expense of a trial. He also pointed out that, because of the tremendous backlog of criminal cases, such a trial might be delayed by as much as a year while the suspect lingered in jail. During the time that Bohanon conducted the interviews, sixteen suspects decided to plead guilty. At the end of two weeks, Bohanon returned to Seminole to open a sub–county attorney's office.

Along with the oilmen, the oil discoveries in Seminole County predictably had attracted the more nefarious elements of society. "Seminole was," Bohanon would remember, "a mecca for prostitutes, bootleggers, narcotics peddlers, thieves, murderers and gamblers. Bishop's Alley, an area occupying four blocks at the north end of Seminole's main street, was dominated by pool halls, beer joints, dance halls, gambling dens and brothels." In these characteristics, Seminole was typical of other eastern Oklahoma oil boomtowns. Historian James Green says of such towns during the period that "bootlegging, gambling, and other 'vice' ran rampant."[25]

In Seminole, establishments such as the Blue Heaven, the Palace, and the Mule Skinner operated twenty-four hours a day and attracted the rowdier elements of the oil field community. Bohanon once walked out of his office in time to see a policeman gunned down with his own weapon. During his tenure as assistant county attorney, Bohanon filed an average of one murder case a week.

At the time, assistant county attorneys were allowed to have their own civil practices to supplement their salaries. Bohanon's practice grew rapidly, and he resigned from the county attorney's office after less than a year. By July 1929 he was sufficiently successful to decide to take on a partner.

On July 4, 1929, Bohanon ran into A. P. ("Fish") Murrah, a friend from OU, as Murrah was admiring Bohanon's new Nash. The pair drove over to Grace's Beer House to catch up. Bohanon had met Grace professionally while he was assistant county attorney, and she boasted that he was one of her favorite persons. After half an hour, she informed them that their "time was up" and that they would have to leave. Otherwise, the sheriff might notice Bohanon's new car parked outside and arrest the pair for violation of the state's prohibition laws. Although the law against consumption of alcoholic beverages was most often winked at by local authorities in Seminole, the sheriff would have loved to have caught a former assistant prosecutor in its violation.

Purchasing a beer each to go, Bohanon and Murrah drove out into the country. Under the cool shade of a tree on a hot Independence Day, the partnership of Murrah & Bohanon was born. It was the latter's idea to place Murrah's name first on the letterhead. Although it had been Bohanon who had been in search of a partner for his profitable legal practice, he was, at the time, more interested in the oil business. If his sideline of selling oil and gas leases proved successful, he planned to leave the law and enter oil drilling and production.

The new partnership grew rapidly. Murrah and Bohanon worked tirelessly, sleeping in their office over a justice of the peace court that operated day and night, never closing. Soon they found that most of their practice was before the state industrial commission and the courts in Oklahoma City. Therefore, in late 1931 the firm moved to offices in the Hightower Building in downtown Oklahoma City. Despite the Depression, their practice and oil dealings on the side prospered, and in 1933 they sold their oil and gas interests for seventy-five thousand dollars. This gave Bohanon sufficient security to buy a new car and home and to

marry Marie Swatek, daughter of prominent local con-
tractor and developer Matthew Anton Swatek.[26]

With the profits from their oil ventures, Murrah and
Bohanon also began to get involved in Oklahoma politics. Although participation in the political process
was then, as now, an accepted way for lawyers to gain
visibility, make contacts, and thus build a practice,
one of Bohanon and Murrah's first involvements grew
out of the desire of several young lawyers in Oklahoma
City to elect younger judges to the Oklahoma County
District Court. In 1934 they joined forces to support
three candidates for the judiciary. They worked hard,
and all three candidates were elected. It is, in fact,
a small irony in the career of Luther Bohanon that
early on he successfully worked to get younger judges
elected to the state judiciary and that later he would be
deemed unfit by the American Bar Association to serve
as a judge because he was too old.

The same year that Bohanon and Murrah became
embroiled in judicial elections, Josh Lee, a professor of
public speaking at the University of Oklahoma School
of Law, asked his old friend Luther Bohanon to support him in his race for the U.S. House of Representatives from Oklahoma's Fifth District. Together with
Murrah and Royce Savage, Bohanon planned Lee's
campaign, expending substantial time and money in
the effort. Lee won handily, and his three former students, Savage, Murrah, and Bohanon, earned themselves a nickname, the "Rover Boys." All three Rover
Boys would ultimately sit on the federal bench.[27]

Two years later, as his first term in the House of
Representatives was coming to an end, Lee decided to
run for the U.S. Senate. The Rover Boys again ran the
campaign. Murrah and Bohanon practiced law by day
and campaigned endlessly at night and on weekends.

The young lawyer taking a break from his practice with wife, Marie, at the 1939 New York World's Fair. The man on the left is friend Weldon Hall.

Through their efforts, the story of Josh Lee, member of Congress, teacher, ordained Baptist minister, and author, was told across the state. Despite the fact that his single term in the House was his only political experience, Lee finished first out of a field of eight in the Democratic primary, running well ahead of E. W. Marland, prominent oil executive, former New Deal member of Congress and incumbent governor and even farther ahead of the incumbent, Senator Thomas P. Gore, an institution in both Oklahoma politics and the Senate.

Thomas Pryor Gore was Oklahoma's first U.S. Senator, sent to Washington in 1907 along with noted Cherokee Robert L. Owen. He was the senior member of the same family that would send Albert Gore and Albert Gore, Jr., to the Senate from Tennessee (and the latter to the vice presidency). It would also produce playwright Gore Vidal.

Although Lee had outdistanced second-place finisher Marland by almost 47,000 votes, the crowded field meant that the election was thrown into a runoff. Three weeks later, he defeated Marland 301,259 votes to 186,999. In Oklahoma in the 1930s, winning the Democratic nomination was tantamount to winning the election, and Lee went on to defeat his Republican opponent in November by a margin of two-to-one.

Then, as now, one of the prerogatives of a U.S. Senator was to recommend to the president individuals to fill vacancies in the federal judiciary in their home state. As one author has explained:

Routinely the senator in office of the same party as the President made the selection, which was presented to the Attorney General, who formally passed the name on to the

President. During all but a few instances both Oklahoma senators have been from the same party. From this has developed a pattern of taking turns in making the selection. During presidential administrations in which both senators are members of the President's opposition party senatorial courtesy is suspended. The President then looks to other sources for the recommendation.[28]

In 1936, Congress created a fourth judgeship to ease the growing burden on Oklahoma's courts, a roving position covering all three of the state's judicial districts. Senator Gore, in the midst of a hotly contested reelection campaign, refrained from filling the newly created vacancy, realizing the potential of his offending large numbers of voters with any selection. When Gore was defeated, the opportunity to recommend the appointment devolved to his successor. Lee chose Murrah, the Rover Boy most interested in the position, as his nominee. President Franklin Roosevelt, who had supported Lee over both Gore and personal friend Marland, complied with the request. Murrah resigned as Bohanon's law partner and took his seat as a federal judge in March 1937.[29] At thirty-three he was the youngest federal judge in the United States.

Years later, Murrah would recall that when he withdrew from their partnership and handed Bohanon his key to the office, Luther said, "Your Honor, this is the last time that I will ever say, 'Your Honor,' to you. I don't have to make a living practicing law in your Court."[30]

In 1938, Bohanon's political activities led to another enduring friendship, one that would lead directly to his own appointment to the bench. That year, Bohanon worked on the successful gubernatorial campaign of Leon ("Red") Phillips. During the election, he worked

Captain Luther Bohanon, Judge Advocate General's Corps, Headquarters, Army Air Force Technical Training Command, Denver, Colorado, December 4, 1943.

closely with a young oilman named Robert S. Kerr.[31] Bohanon's relationship with Kerr and Kerr's brother, Aubrey, would deepen over the years, and when a vacancy occurred on the federal bench in 1960, Kerr, by then a U.S. senator from Oklahoma, would recommend his old friend.

In April 1942, Bohanon was offered a captain's commission in the Judge Advocate General's Corps of the U.S. Army Air Corps. While he considered it his duty to serve his country during wartime, he was involved heavily in Josh Lee's reelection bid at the time. His wife Marie, though wholly behind the war effort, also objected, stating her need to have her husband at home. After much discussion and soul searching, Bohanon agreed to accept the commission only on the condition that he could delay his entry into the service until after the Democratic primary in July.[32] Lee was the incumbent senator, and the request was honored.

Lee won the primary, easily outdistancing nine opponents. But without the last of his Rover Boys, Savage having assumed the federal bench in 1940 and Bohanon having gone into the service, Lee lost to Republican E. H. Moore in the general election.

Despite the fact that he would have been exempted from service because of his age, Bohanon was determined to serve. He was ordered to Miami, Florida, to attend Officer Candidate School. Upon graduation, he was assigned to Camp Kearns in Utah. There, Luther Bohanon, who had once been absent without leave himself when in the National Guard at Fort Sill and who, by his own admission, preferred kitchen police to drill, was appointed trial judge advocate, charged with prosecuting all camp violations. He averaged five disciplinary actions daily, ranging from absence without leave and theft to fighting and insubordination.

In April 1943, Colonel Neal D. Franklin, chief of the Judge Advocate Department of the Army Air Force (AAF) Western Technical Training Command, toured Camp Kearns to inspect the activities of the judge advocate's office and to investigate the unusually high number of troops incarcerated in the brig there under the provost marshal. During the course of his inspection, the colonel asked Bohanon if he was happy with his assignment at Camp Kearns. With the self-assured candor—some would say brashness—that he had displayed throughout his life, Captain Bohanon replied that he felt that his duties were far below his capabilities and that he would like a transfer. The conversation resulted in Bohanon's transfer to Colonel Franklin's staff at the AAF Technical Training Command in Denver, Colorado. He remained with Franklin for the duration of the war, first in Denver and later in Fort Worth.

Upon his discharge in October 1945, Bohanon returned to Oklahoma City and resumed his legal practice with Lynn Adams and Bert Barefoot. The partnership thrived, and soon the partners were earning salaries in excess of one hundred thousand dollars a year, representing such influential clients as Hughes Tool Company and Armand Hammer's Occidental Petroleum. "Of course," writes Bohanon, "our relationship [with these clients] was that of local counsel." An exception was Kerr-McGee Corporation, owned by Bohanon's old friend Bob Kerr, for which they did a great deal of work. When Lynn Adams left the partnership in 1954, at Bohanon's urging, he became chief attorney for the energy concern.

One of the cases awaiting Bohanon and Barefoot upon their return from military duty was *Otoe and Missouria Tribe of Indians* v. *United States*. The case

had actually begun in 1939 but had been put on hold
with the United States' entry into World War II. As the
first case to deal with the question of compensability for aboriginal title to Indian lands, the Otoe and
Missouria claim would become the leading case in
American Indian jurisprudence.[33] As with other such
claims, it would drag on for years and would, in fact,
not be fully adjudicated until well after Bohanon had
assumed the bench.

In February 1939, Baptiste ("Bat") Shunatona, a full-
blood Otoe and Missouria and a classmate of Bohanon
in law school, approached Bohanon and asked him to
join in a case that Shunatona predicted "would revolu-
tionize federal Indian claims." The idea appealed to
Bohanon, and he agreed to visit the tribal council near
Red Rock to discuss "the significance of challenging
current legal practices concerning Indian land claims."

Bohanon explained to the council that before any legal action could proceed, he would need a written contract with the tribe, approved either by the Secretary of
the Interior Harold Ickes or by John Collier's Bureau
of Indian Affairs (BIA), authorizing his firm to undertake work on behalf of the tribe. Bohanon gave them a
contract he had drafted, and the council said that they
would take it under advisement.

In fact, tribe and attorneys were likely to find a sympathetic ear with either Ickes or Collier. Both had been
advocates of Indian rights for many years. In 1923,
Ickes had written of the history of white treatment of
America's indigenous peoples: "A more moving tale
of wrongs wantonly committed and proposed against a
peaceful, law-abiding and self-respecting group of people I have never listened to. The story . . . , if spread
broadcast throughout the country, ought to make every decent American's face burn with shame for the in-

juries that have been and are proposed to be committed in the names of his fellow citizens." Collier was a founder of the American Indian Defense Association in the 1920s. His appointment at the BIA marked a distinct departure in that, unlike his predecessors, he saw it as his job to protect and act as advocate for American Indians. Together with Ickes, he would help forge the Indian New Deal. In fact, reading T. H. Watkins's biography of Ickes, one especially is struck by the similarities in the backgrounds of Ickes and Bohanon which combined to create men of similar outlook and temperment. In particular, both shared pious mothers who deeply influenced their beliefs. Naomi Bliven, writing of Ickes, states, "It's obvious that in his political career he applied the moral rigor and intensity of his mother's faith to secular issues."[34]

Two months passed with no word from the tribe concerning the representation. Puzzled, Bohanon contacted Bat Shunatona, who informed him that the council wanted the lawyers to host a tribal dinner, which would allow them to prove their friendship and to demonstrate that they considered the Indians to be their equals. Shunatona stated that they were to purchase a thousand-pound steer, which the tribe would slaughter and cook in the traditional Indian manner. Concerned about the propriety of such a request, Bohanon contacted the BIA and was informed that it was sanctioned by both the bureau and the American Bar Association (ABA). He was also informed that attorneys for Indians were required to advance all costs of prosecuting claims; in the event that a claim was successful, the lawyer would recoup his or her out-of-pocket costs, but if the claim failed, he or she would lose all funds which had been advanced.

When the time came for the dinner, more than one

hundred Indians, including members of neighboring tribes, assembled. After the meal, the group returned to the Red Rock Agency, where Chief Francis Pipestem put the matter before the tribe. He described the proposed contract and asked if there were any objections. Upon hearing none, he executed the contract.

In his unpublished autobiography, Judge Bohanon says of the *Otoe and Missouria* case:

The case was revolutionary. Previously, the various Indians which had sought legal redress had little success in the Court of Claims. Prior legal decisions had held that Indian title to land granted no legal rights against the United States government and the extinguishment by treaty of Indian land titles was not based on legal obligations. As a result, and because it was not possible for Indians to seek relief through the courts without the federal government granting permission for a suit to be filed, all previous cases generally were based on the extension of the jurisdiction of the Court of Claims to cover certain Indian claims or a special congressional bill granting the right to try a specific claim before the Court of Claims.

The contract between us and the Otoes and Missourias represented a drastic change in the dealings of the federal government with Native Americans. We were preparing the first case involving the question of compensability of aboriginal title to Indian lands. It would be our task to prove that the Otoes and Missourias had lived in their ancestral homeland to the exclusion of all other Indians, and that the neighboring tribes recognized their claim to the ownership of their land.[35]

The contract had a term of five years. Therefore, Bohanon and his colleagues had only until 1944 to prove their case. Bohanon immediately began to work to get the necessary enabling legislation through the U.S. Congress, contacting A. S. ("Mike") Monroney, the member of Congress from Oklahoma's Fifth District, and Senator John William Elmer Thomas.[36]

First elected in 1926, Elmer Thomas would serve twenty-four years in the Senate until defeated for the Democratic nomination in 1950 by Monroney. Despite the fact that he had once been a member of the Ku Klux Klan, he was one of the most respected members of the U.S. Senate ever from Oklahoma, serving as head of the Agriculture Committee and as chair of the Military Affairs Subcommittee. An advocate of Indian rights, he worked closely with Collier's BIA. Later he would use his power as one of the most senior members of the Appropriations Committee to secure authorization for Robert Kerr's pet project, the Arkansas River Navigation Project. He was, in many ways, Kerr's role model for what a U.S. senator could and should be.[37]

While Bohanon worked with Oklahoma's congressional delegation, as chairman of the Oklahoma Democratic Platform Committee and the state's delegate to the Platform Committee of the Democratic National Convention in 1940 he also was able to obtain a plank in the party's presidential platform favoring "the enactment of legislation creating an Indian claims commission for the special purpose of entertaining and investigating claims presented by all Indian groups, bands and tribes, in order that our Indian citizens may have their claims against the government considered, adjusted and finally settled at the earliest possible date." He also worked closely with Herbert K. Hyde and Earl Warren of the Committee on Resolutions at the Republican National Convention to persuade the GOP to pledge itself to "an immediate and final settlement of all Indian claims between the government and the Indian citizenship of the nation."[38]

Unfortunately, just as it appeared that headway was being made, the Japanese attacked Pearl Harbor. Nonessential government agencies were transferred out of Washington as the capital shifted to a war footing. The BIA itself was moved to Chicago and reduced to a skeletal staff. Domestic legislation was frozen until the end of the war. In 1944, although the Republicans kept the platform plank on settlement of Indian claims and, in fact, added the sentence, "We will take politics out of the administration of Indian affairs," the Democrats, despite Bohanon's urging, watered down their 1940 plank to a general endorsement of humanitarian legislation and social justice.[39]

With the end of the war, domestic programs again dominated the public agenda. Congress passed the Indian Claims Commission Act of 1946, creating an Indian Claims Commission to hear and decide all tribal claims concerning land ceded to the U.S. government.[40] As soon as the act was signed by President Truman, Bohanon asked for the rules, regulations, and trial procedures required to be established by the legislation. The tribe's contract with Bohanon and Shunatona had expired; on April 18, 1947, however, they signed a second contract similar to the first. And ten days later, on August 28, the tribe filed its petition with the Indian Claims Commission, alleging that they illegally had been deprived of their ancestral lands.

The case was the eleventh filed but the first to be heard. Thus began an eighteen-year court battle involving two centuries of Otoe and Missouria history. Barefoot, Bohanon, and Adams "came to appreciate the axiom that an Indian lawyer should live to be as old as Methuselah, have the patience of Job, and the wisdom of Solomon."[41]

Ultimately the Otoes and Missourias prevailed, and on August 13, 1965, Mike Monroney, then a U.S. senator, introduced legislation which appropriated $3,464,325 to settle their claim. The lawyers received 10 percent of the settlement plus reimbursement of $40,000 in expenses. Although, by the time of the settlement, Bohanon had resigned from the case to become a judge, he would not have been predisposed to take another such case. "I never worked so long and so hard on a lawsuit," he declared.[42]

As the litigation surrounding the Otoe and Missouria claim was winding down, Bohanon became involved in another complex case that was to have a far-reaching effect on Oklahoma's judiciary long after Bohanon himself had become a judge: *Tyree* v. *Selected Investments Corporation*.

In early 1958, the plaintiff filed suit against Selected Investments, an Oklahoma-based, diversified investment company. The complaint alleged that the corporation's financial condition required court supervision and asked that four receivers be appointed. Bohanon was named attorney for two of the receivers. Soon thereafter, Ernst & Ernst prepared an audit of the firm's financial records which showed a shortfall of approximately twelve million dollars in assets. Bohanon asked that the audit be made public, but the corporation's officers refused, declaring that it would be made public "over our dead bodies." Bohanon then secured, through an ex parte action, an order directing Ernst & Ernst to publish their audit. The revelation of the shortage forced Selected Investments into reorganization, and Bohanon was appointed attorney for the trustee in the bankruptcy case. His investigation, on behalf of the trustee, culminated in a hearing on March 17, 1958, which he would often describe later as his "golden hour in the courtroom."[43] The hearing would uncover a web of mismanagement, bribery, and corruption and touch off a probe by the Internal Revenue Service (IRS).

Bohanon discovered that two hundred thousand dollars had been withdrawn from Selected Investment's trust account by its president, Hugh Carroll. He also discovered that ten days after the withdrawal the Supreme Court of Oklahoma handed down a decision, in the case of *Selected Investments* v. *Oklahoma Tax Commission*, wherein the court overturned a lower court's decision unfavorable to Selected Investments and granted them a judgment in the amount of one-half million dollars.

William A. Berry, justice on the Oklahoma Supreme Court from 1959 until 1978, stated that when he took to the bench the year after the *Selected Investments* decision, he believed that the majority of the justices were dishonest. He writes, "It had been alleged for years among the state's legal profession that cases won on sound reasoning at the trial court level were overturned at the appellate level for no apparent reason." Despite such allegations, however, no one had the courage, states Berry, to call those involved to account. This was understandable, especially if only two or three justices were involved in the presumed sale of judicial decisions. Not only would it most likely be a case of one person's word against another, but, in Oklahoma, it would quickly become a political issue. As Justice Berry writes:

Because of the dominance of the Democratic Party in state politics, the majority of justices, as other statewide office-holders, were Democratic candidates. [In fact,] only four Republicans had served on the Supreme Court. Thus by sheer numbers involved, any exposure of corruption would fall more heavily on the Democratic Party. Faced with this potential embarrassment and the potential repercussions against other Democratic candidates, state officials were hesitant to take any action, unless the corruption was so blatant it could not be ignored.[44]

During the March 1958 hearing on the Selected Investments bankruptcy, Bohanon, through some spry legal gymnastics, managed to get Carroll on the witness stand to answer questions about the withdrawal of two hundred thousand dollars. Carroll testified that he had withdrawn the money to buy oil properties in Canada. He stated that he had given most of the funds to a French–Canadian named Pierre LaVal. LaVal had subsequently, it appeared, absconded with the money, for Carroll had not heard from him since giving him the cash. Carroll said that he did not know if LaVal was living or dead and that he felt as though he had "just bought the Brooklyn Bridge."[45]

All of Carroll's assertions proved to be false. Pierre LaVal, the Canadian who had taken French leave with Selected Investment's funds, was a product of Carroll's imagination. The name itself was, in fact, nothing more than a corruption of Pierre Laval, prominent French politician of the 1930s and 1940s who served as premier during the Vichy government. It was probably seized upon unconsciously by Carroll as the only French-sounding name of which he could think. Given, however, the duplicitous character of the real Laval, one must wonder whether the choice of name for his fabrication was not more or less deliberate.[46]

These circumstances gave substance to the belief that the mysterious $200,000 was in fact a bribe to some member or members of the Oklahoma Supreme

Court. Bohanon challenged the "cloak of secrecy and party loyalty" that rested on the court. According to Justice Berry, "His questioning of Hugh Carroll in open court started the pebble rolling downhill that triggered a landslide. Once the story was exposed, numerous other federal and state officials became involved; however, it was Bohanon's actions that initiated the investigation. . . . It took tremendous personal courage for a practicing attorney to do what he did. If the allegations had not been sustained, he would face an impossible task of practicing law within the state." As the investigation continued, it was determined that $150,000 was actually given as a bribe.[47]

When the reorganization of Selected Investments was completed and left the jurisdiction of the court in late 1958, Bohanon contacted the IRS and presented them with the original two-hundred-thousand-dollar note and check, the trial court's judgment against the company for four hundred thousand dollars, and a copy of the Oklahoma Supreme Court's opinion reversing the trial court in the Oklahoma tax case. Although it took from 1958 until 1965, the IRS's inquiry led to discovery of sale of judicial decisions by three of the state supreme court's nine justices. Two of the three were convicted in 1965 of income tax evasion and sentenced to prison. The third was impeached and removed from office after a trial by the state senate.

Only once before, in 1929, had the credibility of the court been challenged. In that year, impeachment charges were voted by the state House of Representatives against the chief justice and two other members of the court. Although the charges were not sustained by the Senate, they did taint the court, and all but one of the justices either did not seek reelection or were rejected by voters when their terms expired.

Throughout this period Bohanon continued to work in public affairs. He headed his church's committee to build a new sanctuary and parsonage. He also worked as attorney for one of the contractors involved in the Oklahoma City–Atoka Water Project, which helped pave the way for the creation of Lake Stanley Draper, a project necessitated by Oklahoma City's rapid postwar growth and which assured it an adequate water supply "well into the following century."

Bohanon considered work on the Lake Draper project part of his civic responsibility. He has always been a strong believer in public service and in giving back to the state which he feels has given him so much. It is in keeping with another credo by which he has tried to guide his life: "It is impossible to be just if one is not generous."[48]

Soon after completion of his work on the project, Bohanon was nominated by his old friend, Senator Robert S. Kerr, for the position of U.S. district judge. Although eager for the appointment, he was personally saddened to dissolve his partnership with Bert Barefoot, Jr., a relationship he described as "the best working partnership of my professional life." With the nomination and confirmation, he ended thirty-four years of legal practice, long enough to be a career in itself. Subsequent events would prove, however, that Luther Bohanon's legal career was just beginning.

Chapter III

The Judge

ROBERT Kennedy, whose job it was as attorney general under Presidents Kennedy and Johnson to recommend judicial nominations to the president, could never, it is said, understand why anyone would want to be a judge. Being a judge meant that you were "out of the fight." "It's so boring, isn't it?" he once inquired.[1] By contrast, Judge Bohanon would write, "I believe every lawyer in my day and time hoped he would be a federal judge for the honor and opportunity to serve the public in a very high calling."

Luther Bohanon's opportunity came in 1960, thirty-three years after he was admitted to the bar. The presidential election that year pitted John Kennedy, moderate Democrat from Massachusetts, against incumbent Republican Vice President Richard Nixon. At the same time, Bohanon's longtime friend Robert Kerr was up for reelection to the Senate. Because Kennedy was a Catholic and Kerr a staunch Baptist in an overwhelmingly Protestant state, many of Kerr's advisors urged him not to endorse or publicly support the presidential candidate. They well remembered 1928, when Catholic Al Smith lost Oklahoma by 179,000 votes. Kerr sought, in turn, to allay their fears by pointing out that Lyndon Johnson, Kerr's candidate for the Democratic nomination and Kennedy's choice for vice president, would guarantee that Kennedy "would at all times place his duty to his country first and not in response to or directly from any religious hierarchy."[2]

In fact, Kerr had attempted to dissuade Johnson from running with Kennedy. He hyperbolically claimed that if the Texas senator considered taking the vice presidency, "I'll go get my long rifle. If you accept, I'll shoot you right between the eyes." Speaker of the House Rayburn, present at the meeting, took Kerr aside. When the two finished speaking, Kerr told his friend, "Lyndon, if Jack Kennedy asked you to be his running mate, and if you don't take it, I'll shoot you right between the eyes."[3]

Despite Kerr's plea to the Kennedy organization that the Massachusetts senator bypass Oklahoma in his campaigning in order to spare Kerr any potential political embarrassment, Kennedy planned a swing through the state in October. Although Kerr had advised Johnson not to run with Kennedy because of the religious question, telling him that he would be ruined in Texas if he ran on the same ticket as a Catholic, Kerr himself now decided to meet the issue head on. Political consultant Martin Hauan chalks this up to political sagacity on Kerr's part. He writes, "The anti-Catholic voters understood Kerr had no other choice since Kennedy was on the scene as a candidate in Oklahoma, while rabid Kennedy followers, mostly staunch Democrats, were mollified enough to vote 'er straight, which included a vote for Bob Kerr."[4]

Introducing the presidential candidate to an overflow crowd at Oklahoma City's Municipal Auditorium, Kerr called Kennedy "a patriotic Catholic

Democrat for President." He told the audience, "Why my Baptist father and my Baptist mother would turn over in their Democratic grave if they thought I would not speak up for my nominee for President."[5]

On election day, the Kennedy-Johnson ticket lost in Oklahoma by more than 160,000 votes. While Kerr retained his senate seat by more than 89,000 votes, he lost counties that he had never before failed to carry by large margins. After the election, Bohanon told Kerr that his endorsement of Kennedy had cost him 50,000 votes. Kerr wearily replied, "No it didn't, Bo. It cost me at least 75,000."[6]

During the campaign, Bohanon had taken time out from working for his friend's reelection to attend the Tenth Circuit Judicial Conference in Boulder, Colorado, and to visit his former law partner A. P. Murrah, now the chief judge of the Tenth Circuit Court of Appeals. While at the convocation, he ran into an old friend from the army. In his autobiography, Bohanon would identify the friend only as "K.G.," but the man's name was Gerald B. Klein. Klein, a Republican attorney from Tulsa, was presiding officer of the Oklahoma ABA and a member of the ABA committee on the judiciary for the Tenth Circuit; as such, it was he who investigated candidates for the bench and passed on their qualifications.[7]

Klein reminded Bohanon that the incoming president would fill a vacancy created when District Judge William Wallace had died in an automobile accident in June. He said that, as a Republican, he had a good chance of getting the appointment if Nixon were elected. He would, however, need the support of the powerful Senator Kerr, and he asked Bohanon to use his influence with his longtime friend on Klein's behalf. On the other hand, he continued, should Kennedy win, Bohanon would almost certainly be the nominee, and, in that event, Klein would see to it that he had no problem being approved by the ABA. The implications of his friend's words shocked the moralistic Bohanon, and he turned down the proposition.

After the election, in April 1961, at the urging of his brother Aubrey, Senator Kerr called Bohanon to his office in Oklahoma City and told him that he was the senator's selection to fill the vacancy created by Wallace's death. Not entirely surprised, but nonetheless flattered, Bohanon said that he would accept the appointment. "You know," Kerr said, "the FBI will be called to make a thorough examination of your life and any trouble you may have been in." Bohanon said that he was familiar with the procedure and assured the senator that the bureau would find no black marks on his record. In a few days, Kerr submitted the recommendation to Attorney General Robert Kennedy.

By the terms of a 1953 agreement, the Justice Department submitted all nominations for the federal bench to the ABA's Standing Committee on the Federal Judiciary for evaluation. The committee, of which Gerry Klein was a member, came back with an "unqualified" rating for Bohanon. Although not legally bound by the ABA's decision, both Nixon and Kennedy had agreed during the campaign not to appoint anyone whom the bar association deemed unfit, continuing a policy established by President Eisenhower. The rating was enough for Attorney General Kennedy, no friend of Kerr's, to oppose the nomination.[8]

The Justice Department and the ABA were now both against Bohanon's appointment. Assistant Attorney General Byron ("Whizzer") White and William Geoghegan informed Kerr. According to Kerr's biographer, "with an impressive 'due bill' for handling six

major parts of Kennedy's 1961 legislative program—
the highway bill, revision of aid to dependent children
under Social Security, the temporary increase in the
federal debt limit, water and air pollution legislation,
expansion of unemployment compensation, and funds
for the space program—Kerr was astonished when
the Justice Department refused to act" on Bohanon's
appointment. He told White and Geoghegan, "Young
men, I was here a long time before you came. I'm going to be here a long time after you go. I stand by my
recommendation."[9]

White delivered the attorney general's request that
Kerr withdraw the nomination and submit three
names. Kerr replied that the three names were "Bohanon, Bohanon, and Bohanon." If President Kennedy
were unwilling to extend him this courtesy, "Kennedy
had better get himself another boy."[10] The implica-
tion was clear that unless Bohanon's nomination were
made, the administration could forget major portions
of its legislative agenda.

With the departure of Lyndon Johnson, Kerr was
widely recognized to be the most powerful and domineering man in the Senate. Many who knew him,
including Clark Clifford and Eugene McCarthy, recall
him as ruthless. Judge Bohanon prefers, however, the
adjective "domineering." He writes, "He was domineering but was friendly with all those he dominated.
It was his policy to help any and everybody that needed
help, and he sometimes asked favors of those he had
helped."[11] All agree that the title "Uncrowned King of
the United States Senate" was not a hollow epithet.

Most important, Kerr was the second-ranking Democrat on the Senate Finance Committee, and even Attorney General Kennedy was forced to acknowledge
that he was the only one who could handle the com-

mittee's reactionary chairman, Harry Byrd of Virginia, with regard to the administration's tax proposals. The younger Kennedy flatly said, "The one friend we had to obtain passage of all bills dealing with finance and taxes was Kerr because Byrd was chairman of that committee and was going to oppose any legislation that was suggested by President Kennedy." It was a common joke in the cloakroom that "what Kerr wants, Kennedy gets."[12]

Tax legislation immediately stalled. The president sent Bobby Baker, secretary to the Senate majority and a close friend of Vice President Johnson, to find out what the problem was. If anyone could get to the root of the problem, the president felt, it was Baker; he was one of Kerr's closest friends and thought of the senator "like a father." Kerr could be vicious. "Poisonous as a scorpion's tail," one Senate colleague called his tongue. All who knew him agree on his prowess in debate and his tart tongue. Kerr bluntly told Baker, "Tell him [President Kennedy] to get his dumb fuckin' brother to quit opposing my friend."[13]

Determined not to yield, but persuaded by Kerr that his position was untenable without personal knowledge of Bohanon's qualifications, in July, Attorney General Kennedy sent John Seigenthaler, his administrative assistant at the Justice Department, to Oklahoma to investigate the nominee. Kerr welcomed the visit. He stated, "I was happy to see them go to Oklahoma. I was frank to tell them they weren't in a very tenable position to do anything other than follow my recommendation. . . . I was sure since they decided to do that they would find my recommendation fully justified."[14]

Although, according to some, the investigators were "unimpressed," both the FBI and Seigenthaler reported back favorably concerning Bohanon's qualifications. They stated that the ABA's opposition was based on misinformation and recommended that the attorney general disregard the bar association's evaluation.[15] In August, Assistant Attorney General White visited Oklahoma City and Tulsa to confer with Klein and the ABA.

Kerr enlisted the aid of Oklahoma Governor J. Howard Edmondson, a close Kennedy confidant, to try to get some movement. Handsome, young, and vigorous, Edmondson and Kennedy were kindred spirits. Edmondson had been the only Oklahoma politician to support Kennedy for the Democratic nomination in 1960. Years later, on January 1, 1963, the day Senator Kerr died, Edmondson and Kennedy were together at the Orange Bowl, watching Oklahoma play Alabama. Kennedy, in fact, was influential in persuading the Oklahoma governor to arrange his own appointment to succeed the late Kerr.[16]

Still, nothing happened. On August 9, the *Daily Oklahoman,* Oklahoma's largest newspaper, reported, "Kerr's political plum was slowly becoming a prune." Vexed that the issue was no longer Luther Bohanon but his own prestige, Kerr announced that if the president appointed anyone other than Bohanon, he would block Senate confirmation.[17]

In an effort to break the "logjam at Justice," Rex Hawks, a former U.S. marshal during the Truman administration and another stalled Kerr appointee, went to see Whizzer White. Hawks was one of Kerr's key operatives, along with Oklahoma Speaker of the House J. D. McCarty and H. I. Hinds (also an Edmondson employee). He reportedly attended meetings at which the senator did not want to be seen personally. The assistant attorney general assured Hawks that his own re-appointment as a federal marshal was not the problem. He reiterated that if Senator Kerr would simply make another recommendation for the vacant judgeship, everything would proceed smoothly.[18]

Hawks reported the conversation directly to Kerr at his Capitol Hill office. The senator listened and then without any sign of emotion picked up the telephone and called the president, requesting an appointment for 5:30 that afternoon. The next day, August 17, the White House issued a press release announcing President Kennedy's intention to appoint Luther Bohanon to the federal bench. The day that Bohanon's nomination reached the Capitol, the Senate passed the controversial Foreign Assistance Act of 1961 with Kerr's active support.[19]

Anne Hodges Morgan, in her biography of Kerr, writes:

It was unlikely that President Kennedy was aware of the serious nature of the quarrel between his brother and the Senator. Preoccupied with the Vienna summit and the increasing Soviet pressure which resulted in the Russians sealing the borders of East Germany, patronage matters were of minor concern. But he quickly recognized the repercussions if Kerr were not appeased. In terms of political power, the Oklahoman was infinitely more important to the President than the American Bar Association.[20]

He also probably knew that, as flexible as Kerr could be in political matters, he would never renege on a promise to a friend and to his brother, a sentiment with which a Kennedy was completely familiar.

The Senate promptly confirmed Bohanon. It had become a personal matter between Kerr and Robert Kennedy. In the end, it was said, Kerr "litèrally dragged"

Bohanon "onto the bench" himself. He had succeeded in forcing the Kennedys to "come to heel."[21]

Unfortunately, the deep embarrassment caused to Bohanon by the ABA rating was not yet over. He was scheduled to be sworn in on September 7, 1961. According to the judge, "As the judges who were to participate in the swearing in gathered in the library, a note was sent in by K. G. [Klein] requesting to be heard during the ceremony. Though the ABA had not protested my appointment to the Senate Committee, K. G. [Klein] wanted to state in open court during my swearing in that it was the ABA's position that I was not qualified." Klein explained that the ABA felt Bohanon to be too old, at age fifty-nine, to be appointed. Further, although he had been a prosecutor and had some litigation experience, Bohanon was, from the bar association's point of view, essentially a corporate lawyer and not suited for the federal bench in that he did not have the "substantial amount of trial experience" demanded by the bar organization. In fact, the ABA's stated policy on age was that no one over sixty should be nominated as a federal judge. The organization was thus not even abiding by its own previously established guidelines.[22]

The Tulsa attorney had not counted on the fact that Judge Murrah, Bohanon's old friend and law partner, was in charge of the ceremony. Royce Savage, the third Rover Boy and now chief justice of the U.S. District Court for the Northern District of Oklahoma, was also present, as was former senator Josh Lee. Murrah summarily dismissed Klein's request, believing that Bohanon and his family had already suffered enough disturbance of mind. Bruce McClelland, vice president of the Oklahoma Bar Association, presented Bohanon to be sworn in, calling him a "distinguished and out-

standing member" of the bar.[23] Robert Kerr and Luther
Bohanon felt fully vindicated.

According to historian Arthur Schlesinger, Robert
Kennedy reported that Bohanon's nomination was the
only judicial appointment on which he and the president were really on opposite sides. The younger Kennedy said:

It was the judge that I felt strongest about, and [Kerr] was really so blatant about it that I really disliked him. I might say
that President Kennedy rather liked him.... He was so effective—I mean the way he operated.... You really have to
balance off. It sounds terrible.... [But] you stand fast on
principle and Kerr doesn't get his judge, and you don't get
any tax legislation. They play as tough and as mean as that.[24]

In the end, Kennedy reported in a taped interview
with Anthony Lewis, perhaps with a degree of self-
justification, that the administration examined Bohanon's credentials and appointed him "in good conscience."[25] Still, they did not expect much from him.

In his biography of Robert Kennedy, Schlesinger
writes, "So Bohanon became a judge—and turned out,
to general surprise, not too bad, at least on civil
rights." Many years later, in a warm letter to the judge,
the historian recalls, "After all the initial clamor, you
turned out to be a pleasant surprise to the Department
of Justice on the bench." He termed Bohanon's career
as a judge to have been "eminent."[26]

Robert Kennedy and Arthur Schlesinger were not
the only ones who were surprised. Frosty Troy, muck-
raking editor of the *Oklahoma Observer*, a liberal
voice amid Oklahoma's primarily conservative press,
wrote:

Tongues clucked in the corporate law firms when Bohanon was nominated for the federal bench, a political appointee of Senator Robert S. Kerr. The American Bar sought
to block his nomination but underestimated Kerr's political
clout with the White House.

Predictions were that he wouldn't be much of a federal
judge, perhaps even a disaster.

He proved instead to be a disaster for segregationists, for
Oklahoma's lock-'em-up Legislature, for those who disdain
the Constitution except when it cuts their way.[27]

During his tenure on the bench, it has been Judge Bohanon's lot to draw the most sensitive and emotional
cases in the modern history of the federal courts in
Oklahoma. Editor Troy believes that it was not acci-
dental: "His judicial zeal gave him little time for the
cozy brother-in-law relationships so common between
judges and lawyers, a milieu that pervades both the
federal and state benches in Oklahoma. It was probably no accident that every time a 'stinker' hit the federal courts, Bohanon was assigned the case." Troy
went on to write, "Pecksniffs who huffed at his lack of
'distinguished credentials' were silenced as his fidelity
to the U.S. Constitution spawned legal courage and
personal integrity rare on the bench or anywhere else
in public life today."[28]

Nowhere were those qualities of courage and integrity more evident than in the 1967 trial of Oklahoma
Speaker of the House J. D. McCarty for income tax evasion. McCarty had been one of Robert Kerr's "most
trusted lieutenants,"[29] and Bohanon had been put on
the bench on the recommendation of Senator Kerr.
Nevertheless Bohanon was selected to try the case.
The matter was of obvious political sensitivity. If Troy
is correct in his assessment that all the "stinkers"

were assigned to Bohanon, then perhaps this was simply one more opportunity for him to fail. Alternatively, perhaps it was felt that, because of their mutual ties to the late senator, Bohanon would be sympathetic to the defense. Both views would be proven incorrect. And the trial was one of the few instances in which Bohanon received immediate kudos inside Oklahoma for the performance of his duties.

McCarty had been a legislator for twenty-six years and speaker of the Oklahoma House of Representatives for three terms. It was said that he "ruled the legislature and two governors." While Kerr was alive, McCarty was the second most powerful man in Oklahoma, and with the senator's sudden death on New Year's Day, 1963, he assumed sole possession of the title of most powerful. Governors alternately feared and courted McCarty and reportedly even placed paid informants within his "knothole gang" in the state legislature. As veteran political consultant Martin Hauan said, "He had a lock on the job [of speaker], until felled by a $12,000 'fee' from the Oklahoma City Chamber of Commerce which he failed to report and couldn't explain to Uncle Sam's ferrets."[30]

McCarty was indicted on April 6, 1967, by a federal grand jury on three counts of income tax evasion and three counts of knowingly signing false tax returns and swearing them to be true. The charges included his failure to report not only the twelve thousand dollars in monthly fees received from the Chamber of Commerce and ten thousand dollars in insurance commissions paid to him in his profession as insurance agent, but also five thousand dollars that he allegedly received in 1961 for influencing a bill concerning horse racing that had been before the legislature.[31]

Bohanon's conduct of the week-long trial in July

1967 was described as "exemplary" and "perfect." If defense attorneys John Moran and James W. Berry hoped that Bohanon would lean toward McCarty, they were mistaken in that hope. He steadfastly refused to inject himself into the proceedings. "He brooked no nonsense, no unnecessary delays. He used the U.S. marshal's staff to closely supervise the jury at all times."[32]

A young Frosty Troy, covering the trial for the *Tulsa Tribune*, was impressed. He wrote that Bohanon presided over the most dignified court he had ever seen. He stated, "His rigid impartiality, stony decorum and judicial efficiency is what the guy must have had in mind when he coined the phrase 'The majesty of the law.'" Although Bohanon's charge to the jury became the basis of McCarty's appeal to the U.S. Supreme Court, the trial made a life-long believer in the judicial system out of Troy. In summing up the trial after the verdict, he said that the McCarty trial proved that "if a judge guides on the law and sticks to good rules of evidence, if the prosecution makes its charges plain and the defense rebuts in clarity, any 12 citizens of average intelligence can draw just conclusions."[33]

McCarty was found guilty on one count each of tax evasion and knowingly signing a false return. He was acquitted on the remaining four counts, including the one relating to the 1961 bribe. In September, Judge Bohanon sentenced him to three years' imprisonment on the evasion charge and an additional three years' probation on the perjury count.[34]

When McCarty's appeals were exhausted in mid-October, 1969, his lawyers asked Bohanon to reconsider the sentence. Bohanon told them that if the former legislator's tax bill, amounting to approximately seventy thousand dollars with penalties and interest, were paid in full, he would consider reducing the sentence. McCarty surrendered himself to federal authorities and began serving his prison term on November 21. The back taxes were paid, and the former speaker spent only a few months in jail.[35]

Praise such as that received for the McCarty trial was given seldom and was ultimately short-lived. Through much of his career, Judge Bohanon has had to endure tremendous opprobrium for his actions. He was repeatedly pilloried in the stocks of public opinion. He resigned from the ABA as a result of their handling of his nomination to the court. He was attacked regularly in the Oklahoma legislature and the press. When property values dropped as result of his school desegregation orders, he was made unwelcome at the church he had helped to build and was forced to leave it. Much of the time he was sustained only by his belief in the absolute rightness of his positions, his family, the power of prayer, and his memories of his dear friend and professor Dean Julien Monnet, who despite threats and personal villification had persisted in upholding principles he believed fundamental to our scheme of government, principles he drilled into his students. "He had to keep his head together," said Larry Meacham, Oklahoma Department of Corrections director and an opponent in Bohanon's battle to reform the state's prison system, "because he didn't have a sympathetic ear in the state."[36]

Eventually, Bohanon's rectitude and doughty devotion to the Constitution won over even many of his critics. Late in his career he was honored by the press, awarded honorary degrees by universities, and lauded by the governors and state politicians who had so often opposed him. In 1979 both chambers of the state legis-

lature formally commended him for his work. The
Oklahoma House of Representatives citation stated:

Judge Luther Bohanon has consistently displayed a courage
few men attain in rare moments of historical crisis, and
that courage has consistently been put into vigorous action
on the side of the disadvantaged, the maltreated, and those
who have no other spokesman; and whose valor has not
been diminished by the hope of gain or the fear of loss, the
Oklahoma House of Representatives proudly recognizes this
unique man's long years of service to the judiciary and to the
people it was designed to serve."

The Senate resolution passed three weeks earlier commended him for his decisions that had sought to effect
some measure of equality for all races and declared
that he had brought hope to the disadvantaged and en-
lightenment and progress to the judiciary.[37]
    It is a mark of Luther Bohanon's powers of survival
that he is now considered the doyen of Oklahoma's
judiciary. In 1990, three separate honors confirmed
this status. In July 1990 the board of trustees of Oklahoma City University unanimously voted to confer
the honorary degree of doctor of laws upon Bohanon. In
a letter, Marian P. Opala, vice chief justice of the Oklahoma Supreme Court, agreed that Bohanon deserved
this tribute for his "courageous judicature in the cause
of equal rights for all Americans." The following October, the board of directors of the Oklahoma City Region of the National Conference of Christians and Jews
informed him that he was to be a recipient of its 1991
Humanitarian Award in recognition of his work on behalf of civil rights and civil liberties. And in November, Judge Bohanon received a letter from Oklahoma

Supreme Court Justice Hardy Summers stating that the Oklahoma City chapter of the prestigious American Inns of Court, an organization for the training and inculcation of young lawyers patterned on the British system of Inns of Court, was renaming itself the Luther Bohanon Inn of Court. In informing the judge of the honor, Justice Summers wrote, "My hope is that each lawyer and law student who passes through the Inn may in some way be touched and enriched by the learning, integrity, courage and grace with which you have conducted yourself professionally. I esteem it an honor to be a part of an Inn which will hereafter bear your name."[38]

Although such honors are personally gratifying to a judge who was once assessed as unfit for the judiciary, making him, as they do, "very happy and proud," they have little to do with Judge Bohanon's self-appraisal. When asked how he wanted to be remembered, he said that he wanted to be recalled as one who let both sides make a full and complete record and decided cases to the best of his ability, according to the law regardless of "which way the chips fell." Plutarch said, "Courage consists not in hazarding without fear, but being resolutely minded in a just cause." Frosty Troy may be correct that that is an apt description of Luther Bohanon's judicial career, but Judge Bohanon has given a better description of a wise federal judge.[39]

These qualities were tested severely in his first case on the bench, *Dowell* v. *Board of Education*.

Chapter IV

The School Board Case

The cases are remanded to the District Courts to take such proceedings and enter such orders and decrees consistent with this opinion as are necessary and proper to admit to public schools on a racially non-discriminatory basis with all deliberate speed the parties to these cases.

BROWN V. BOARD OF EDUCATION,
349 U.S. 294 (1955)

From a study of the evidence in this case, the Court concludes that the Oklahoma City School Board has followed a course of integration as slowly as possible. Our Negro people, business, religious and educational leaders have so far as this record is concerned been completely ignored, and it is their rights that are at long last before this Court. One of the basic foundations of America's strength, and one of the keys to its greatness, is the right to have equal public schools for all our children. The right of each American child to enjoy free equal schools. If any white child were denied such right all would be indignant; why not let it be so with our Negro children.

DOWELL V. BOARD OF EDUCATION,
219 F.Supp. 427 (W.D. Okl. 1963)

THE long struggle of African-Americans for equality under the law is one of the most inspiring, if unfinished, chapters in our nation's history. In that struggle, the school integration cases would be recalled by Jack Greenberg, who, as chief counsel of the NAACP Legal Defense Fund, developed strategy for *Dowell* v. *Board of Education* as the "trench warfare of the civil rights movement."[1]

In October 1961, Dr. Alonzo L. Dowell, an Oklahoma City optometrist, filed suit in the U.S. District Court for the Western District of Oklahoma on behalf of his minor son Robert, who was seeking a transfer from a predominantly black high school to a school that was predominantly white. Judge Bohanon would later describe the ensuing battle as "a sad tale characterized by obduracy, procrastination and deception . . . defiance and bad faith."[2] Thirty years later, he has rendered only now what is perhaps his final opinion in the case.

To understand *Dowell* adequately, it is necessary to review the rather complex history of Oklahoma as a "Jim Crow" state and the efforts of Oklahoma's blacks to overcome that peculiar system of American apartheid.

Because each of the Five Civilized Tribes had, to varying degrees, held slaves, at the end of the Civil War there were thousands of blacks living within the present boundaries of the State of Oklahoma long before any sizeable white population. When slavery was abolished by the postwar Indian treaties of 1866, most of those former slaves of Indians remained to be joined by a "steady influx" of Southern freedmen, primarily from Texas, Louisiana, and Arkansas. By the time of the passage of the Organic Act of May 2, 1890, creating the Oklahoma and Indian territories, the twin territories had a combined total of 22,000 African-American residents, representing 8.4 percent of the then total population.[3]

By 1900 this figure had swelled to 56,000, but increased white immigration had decreased the ratio of blacks to just 7 percent of the population. Historian Danney Goble, in his book *Progressive Oklahoma: The Making of a New Kind of State*, wrote:

Neither territory [Oklahoma or Indian], despite the hopes of its black Boomers, ever became a haven for black aspirations. There was ... a measure of uncertainty and hope as the two races of both territories groped toward defining an acceptable scheme of race relations. In Oklahoma Territory, blacks voted and held office—both appointive and elective—through the territorial years. In some places, and at some times, black and white school children attended integrated public schools. Public accommodations were open to both races as blacks took their places alongside whites in territorial hotels, restaurants, and transportation facilities. Within Indian Territory, the available, if scanty, evidence demonstrates clearly that blacks, both freedmen and immigrants, were deeply involved in politics in several towns, and freedmen voted and held office in some tribal governments.... It also appears that blacks had free access to at least some public facilities in the Indian Territory.

Throughout the 1890s, the fluidity of race relations described by Goble slowly gave way in Oklahoma, as it did elsewhere in the post-Reconstruction South, to the rigid segregation of Jim Crow laws.[4]

In September 1890, Oklahoma Territory's first territorial legislature enacted, after acrimonious debate, the territory's first education bill. The bill left segregation to local option at the county level, allowing local districts to establish separate schools if patrons in the county so opted. This local-option policy remained in effect until 1897. One district in Lincoln County developed, because of the practical constraints of territorial life, perhaps the oddest system in the disgraceful history of Jim Crow: the races sat in adjoining rooms in an abandoned farmhouse; the teacher lectured to both classes simultaneously from the hallway. Although in 1897 new statutes were passed that ended the local-option policy, not until 1901 did the Oklahoma Territory order total segregation of its public schools. According to Goble, "With a new, elaborate statute, the legislature absolutely forbade interracial schooling, including the teaching of one race by members of the other, attached ample enforcement machinery, and provided for a County Separate School Fund to finance the victory of school-boy Jim Crow." Year's later, Judge Bohanon would note, with no small irony, that when he and his family were going to school in Blaine Bottom as the only whites in a school of full-blood Choctaws, it was unlawful for white and African-American children to attend school together.[5]

On June 16, 1906, President Theodore Roosevelt signed the Hamilton Bill into law. The Enabling Act, as it came to be called, authorized admission of Oklahoma and Indian territories as a single state. The act provided that the constitution of the new state should protect its citizens against "distinction in civil or political rights on account of race or color" and that a system of public education should be developed "open to all children of the state." The act went on to specify, however, "this shall not be construed to prevent the establishment and maintenance of separate schools for white and colored children." In response to the permissiveness of the act, the Oklahoma Constitutional Convention included in the state's constitution Article

XIII, which read in part: "Separate schools for white and colored children.—Separate schools for white and colored children with like accommodation shall be provided by the Legislature and impartially maintained. The term 'colored children,' as used in this section, shall be construed to mean children of African descent. The term 'white children' shall include all other children." It was this clause that Judge Bohanon would strike down in *Dowell* in 1963, fifty-six years after its enactment.[6]

When the legislature of the new state convened in December 1907, a local 1929 history notes with obvious pride, the first bills introduced in both houses were measures requiring separate coaches and waiting rooms for African-Americans in all railway facilities. In the years from 1907 until 1941, further laws were passed legislating enforced segregation, including laws mandating separate telephone booths, cemeteries, and even separate boats when fishing. By 1944, Gunnar Myrdal's observation about the Deep South was only slightly less true of Oklahoma, "Segregation is now becoming so complete that the white Southerner practically never sees a Negro except as his servant and in other standardized and formalized caste situations." Although Oklahoma may have been only "on the rim of the South," as journalist Frosty Troy has pointed out, its approach to race relations has always been "Deep South" despite its rhetoric to the contrary.[7]

It should not be thought, however, that Oklahoma's African-Americans during this period merely accepted the continued diminution and abrogation of their constitutional rights. As early as 1898, blacks were seeking redress of grievances in the courts. In 1914, four Oklahoma African-Americans sought to enjoin their state's railway law. The following year, they took on the so-called Grandfather Clause.[8]

This odious law, which in effect allowed only white males to vote, resulted from a political scrap between the state's Republicans and Democrats. When Republicans won three of the congressional house seats from Oklahoma, local Democratic leaders blamed black voters as the cause. The second state legislature, controlled by Democrats, responded by passing a literacy requirement. Election board officials were unfettered in their administration of the required test, and only those whose forebears had been eligible to vote on January 1, 1866, were exempt from the requirement. African-Americans were thus effectively denied the vote because few could meet that standard.

On June 1, 1915, in *Guinn* v. *United States,* after a challenge by Oklahoma blacks, the U.S. Supreme Court struck down the Grandfather Clause. The same local history cited previously with reference to other Jim Crow laws said of *Guinn* and the law's overturning:

Thus ended the first effort to accomplish by subterfuge that which could only be achieved by the exercise of constructive statemanship of the highest order. That a condition which would have abundantly justified a courageous appeal for the rectification of the most monumental blunder of the Reconstruction Period could not justify a measure which was open to the charge of partisan expediency, was not surprising. The question as to the possibility of the permanent endurance of a democracy, the constituent citizenship of which is not of a homogeneous character, is one of grave doubt. In any attempt to find its solution, due regard must be paid to underlying principles; and this, with the adaptability or lack of the same on the part of a questionable element, must eventually outweigh prejudice, sentimentalism and even artificially created rights.[9]

The problem then, at least for some Oklahomans, was the "artificially created rights" of the Fourteenth and Fifteenth amendments and political infighting between political parties rather than denial of equal protection to black citizens.

The principal moving force behind *Guinn* was Roscoe Dunjee, founder and editor of the *Black Dispatch*, Oklahoma City's African-American newspaper. Dunjee was the son of John Dunjee, a slave who had escaped slavery through the Underground Railroad and had gone on to become a Baptist minister. In 1892, the elder Dunjee was sent to Oklahoma by the American Baptist Home Missionary Society. He labored from 1892 until 1902 organizing churches. His work is credited as being the "beginning of organized life among Negroes in Oklahoma City."[10]

Roscoe Dunjee had been taught to believe in equality by his father. Surrounding himself with a cadre of African-American ministers and lawyers for tactical and legal advice, Dunjee became the major factor in Oklahoma's embryonic civil rights movement.[11]

Perhaps the greatest, if most back-handed, compliment received by Dunjee during the early days of the fledgling movement came from William H. Murray, president of Oklahoma's Constitutional Convention and governor during the 1930s. Murray once told a group, "You fellows have been listening to Roscoe Dunjee, and he's a hundred years ahead of his time." George Lynn Cross also pointed out Dunjee's acumen. In 1941, when a state senate committee investigated possible Communist influence in the state, Dunjee was among those called to testify. When asked what he knew about civil rights, the editor replied that he knew enough to know that his were being violated that day.[12]

Dunjee helped found the Urban League of Oklahoma City, one of the first such chapters in a Southern city, and became state president and a national director of the NAACP. No movement of any consequence was started in Oklahoma for a period of forty years without his advice, consent, and, most often, active participation.[13]

Dunjee pushed to get blacks the right to serve on juries. Under his leadership, a number of suits were brought to remove the exclusion. Finally, in 1935 he was successful in *Hollins* v. *Oklahoma*. *Hollins* set the precedent for both state and nation, outlawing the barring of African-Americans from juries.

As World War II drew to a close, Dunjee and James E. Stewart, a member of the national board of directors of the NAACP, decided the time was right to launch a broad attack on Jim Crow in Oklahoma. Realizing the need for ideological underpinnings for tactics to be employed, Dunjee set out to forge a union between his *Black Dispatch* and churches. In her dissertation on the Urban League, Louise Carol Stephens writes: "The press and pulpit joined in what many of the older residents termed, 'a refusal to be politically enslaved by people who had come to the state seeking a larger freedom for themselves.'" Education was to be the first target. According to Harvard law professor Derrick Bell, one of the NAACP Legal Defense Fund (LDF) attorneys on the *Dowell* case, "We civil rights lawyers attacked segregation in public schools because it was the weak link in the 'separate but equal' chain. Our attack worked."[14]

In early September 1945, an NAACP meeting was held in McAlester, Oklahoma, with Thurgood Marshall, the organization's chief counsel, in attendance. When the meeting ended on Saturday, September 3, Marshall announced that it had reached a decision to attack Oklahoma's segregation laws in the courts. Attempts would be made to enroll students at the University of Oklahoma in Norman and at Oklahoma A&M College in Stillwater. The students would attempt to enroll in graduate and professional programs not available at Oklahoma's black institution, Langston University.[15]

The tactics to be followed were thus to be similar to those employed with some success in *Missouri ex rel. Gaines* v. *Canada* in 1938, wherein the U.S. Supreme Court had ruled that either blacks had to be admitted to law school at the University of Missouri or a separate school had to be established at Lincoln University. Although acquiescing in the tactic, Dunjee disagreed, preferring a more direct approach. He thus became the first of the group to publicly call into question the principle of separate but equal. He stated that he opposed separate schools for blacks and whites because they "operate on the theory that one human being is better than another."[16]

On January 14, 1946, Ada Lois Sipuel Fisher, accompanied by Dunjee and W. A. J. Bullock, regional director of the NAACP, presented herself for enrollment at the University of Oklahoma School of Law. University president George L. Cross informed her that he must deny her application because state law forbade admission of blacks. Dunjee listened impassively and then suggested that the president give him a letter saying that Mrs. Fisher had been denied admittance solely based on her race. Cross, a native of South Dakota and no friend of Jim Crow, agreed and dictated the letter in the group's presence. The missive became the basis of a challenge in the courts.[17]

The court test was based on the *Gaines* principle. NAACP attorney Amos Hall argued that Fisher had been denied her right to a separate-but-equal education because no law school for blacks existed in Oklahoma. Dunjee still disagreed. He "made his contrasting position clear to the press from the beginning. He declared that there could be no separate-but-equal education— that equal opportunity could exist only where the same education was available to both races." When Thurgood Marshall agrued the case before the Oklahoma Supreme Court, he elaborated on the theme first expounded by Dunjee, urging that segregation itself amounted to a constitutional infringement, that equality in a segregated system was a "legal fiction," a "judicial myth."[18]

Dunjee and Hall also pressed the case of George McLaurin, who had applied to OU's graduate school. Although in both cases the NAACP met with only limited success, *Sipuel* and *McLaurin* represent two landmark cases that paved the way for the Supreme Court's pronouncements in *Brown* v. *Board of Education*.[19]

It was the *Brown* decision in 1954 that finally provided the instrument by which to break the back of Jim Crow in Oklahoma and throughout the nation. Although Bohanon states that before the *Dowell* case he had never had any particular feelings about the plight of African-Americans or other oppressed groups, he immediately took note of and recognized the importance of the *Brown* decision, believing that educating blacks and whites together was the only road to equality for blacks. Years later he would tell his old acquaintance, Justice Warren, that he believed *Brown* to be the greatest decision in the history of the high court, and he would consider *Dowell* to be his single greatest achievement as a judge. Bohanon recognized that, in *Brown*, African-Americans had before them "a new day—new rights which had for years been denied them—new hopes and expectations."[20]

In *Brown*, the justices declared that "segregation of white and Negro children in the public schools of a State solely on the basis of race, pursuant to state laws permitting or requiring such segregation, denies Negro children the equal protection of the laws guaranteed by the Fourteenth Amendment." Although the ruling struck down the *Plessy* v. *Ferguson* doctrine of separate but equal, it did not specify who would implement the integration of the nation's public schools. This fact led the following year to the so-called *Brown II* decision, wherein the Court reaffirmed the belief that "racial discrimination in public education is unconstitutional" and charged district courts with the task of ensuring desegregation "with all deliberate speed." It had been decided in the deliberations for the *Brown II* decision that the Supreme Court should remand to the district courts to supervise the Court's decree because such courts were "closer to the circumstances of each case, and may be regarded less as interlopers than this Court would be, in exercising direct supervision."[21] *Brown II* also ordered that during the transition from a dual to a unitary school system, the district courts were to retain jurisdiction over the cases to determine "whether the action of the school authorities constitutes good faith implementation of governing constitutional principles."

At the outset, it appeared that integration would proceed smoothly in Oklahoma. Governor Johnston

Murray (1951–55), the son of former Governor William
H. ("Alfalfa Bill") Murray (whose racial opinions were
a constant source of embarrassment to Johnston, a racial moderate), pledged compliance with the Court's
May 17, 1954, order, saying, "Our people have demonstrated that whatever the law is, it will be accepted."
In fact, in her autobiographical account of Oklahoma's
civil rights years, activist Clara Luper praises the
younger Murray and his successor, Raymond Gary, for
their "straight forward and far-sighted leadership" in
urging state citizens to accept the *Brown* decision. For
his part, Gary, though raised in the conservative southeastern corner of Oklahoma, became one of Jim Crow's
staunchest opponents. He maintained, "I grew up in
'Little Dixie'. . . , [but as] an active Baptist and believer
in the Scriptures . . . I have never understood how persons can call themselves Christians and believe that
God made them superior because they were born with
white skin."[22]

F. D. Moon, principal of all-black Frederick Douglass
High School, declared, "In my opinion, this is the decision of the 20th century just as the . . . Dred Scott case
in 1858 was the outstanding decision of the 19th century." Catholic private schools integrated. As Bohanon
recalls, there was little opposition to the *Brown* decisions among the rural Oklahoma school districts. State
officials merely asked for more time to work out the
financial problems of integration. In fact, Thurgood
Marshall praised Oklahoma for its compliance with
the ruling. But, as Judge Bohanon would later write,
"What Marshall did not know was that transfer of
black students to white schools left more than 300
black teachers and administrators without jobs. Until
Brown I and *II* the only nationwide profession for
blacks was education. This was the reason for the high

percentage of masters and doctoral degrees held by black teachers. With no employment available after integration, most of them were forced to move out of state to find other jobs." Bohanon's assessment was correct: the Urban League was forced to focus "much of its attention on helping Negro teachers who have been displaced because of integration of the public schools."[23]

There was no such readiness to comply, however, in the urban areas of Tulsa and Oklahoma City.[24] Thus began the "sad tale" of deception described by Bohanon in *Dowell*.

The Supreme Court may have felt that it was "greasing the skids" of compliance by remanding the task of desegregation to the lower courts, but what the justices failed to recognize was best summarized by Jack Peltason:

The District judge is very much a part of the life of the South. He must eventually leave his chambers and when he does he attends a Rotary lunch or stops at the club to drink with men outraged by what they consider [judicial tyranny]. A judge who makes rulings adverse to segregation is not likely to be honored by testimonial dinners, or to read flattering editorials in the local press, or to partake in the fellowship at the club.[25]

As Derrick Bell states in his book on the elusive quest for racial justice, *And We Are Not Saved*, school boards and their lawyers soon found many devices "to convey a sense of compliance with *Brown*, while in fact the schools remained segregated. . . . Unravelling the seemingly neutral procedures contained in these plans to get at their segregation-maintaining intent proved a challenge for both civil rights lawyers and for many federal judges who were ostracized and abused for carrying out the *Brown* mandate."[26]

In the face of pressures to integrate following the *Brown* decisions, on August 1, 1955, the Oklahoma City School Board approved a "Statement Concerning Integration" asking for the "cooperation and patience" of Oklahoma City residents in the board's "compliance with the law and making the changes that are necessary and advisable." A few district boundaries were changed, but as the statement itself attests, these new lines "consider natural geographic boundaries, such as major traffic streets, railroads, the river, etc." With the beginning of the 1955–56 school term, 300 African-American children, out of a total enrollment of 68,000 students, enrolled at nine formerly segregated schools. Otherwise, the board did nothing, relying on dictum contained in the Supreme Court's opinion in *Briggs* v. *Elliot*, which stated that although it was the courts' duty to strike down segregation laws, they need not mandate integration if it did not occur naturally. It was not in the field of education that the first post-*Brown* victories over segregation would be attained in Oklahoma.[27]

The NAACP launched a voter registration drive which met with impressive success. In 1955 only 40 percent of those African-Americans eligible to vote were registered, and only 30 percent of that number voted. By 1965, 65 percent of those eligible were registered, and an average of 75 percent voted.[28]

In spite of such progress, however, "blacks in Oklahoma City were still systematically excluded from most of its theaters, restaurants, barber and beauty shops and amusements." It was during this period that one of the most significant figures in the struggle for desegregation in Oklahoma emerged. Her name was

Clara Luper, a history teacher at all-black Dunjee High School, named for Roscoe Dunjee. She was also adult advisor to the local NAACP Youth Council.[29]

Deeply influenced by Martin Luther King, Jr., Mrs. Luper wrote a play about him which the Youth Council was asked to perform in New York. While traveling to New York, she and her charges received lunch counter service on an equal basis with whites all through the North. As historian Carl Graves notes, "Enjoying a hamburger at an integrated restaurant was a new experience for most of the youngsters. On the return trip they traveled a southern route, where they faced discrimination once again. After returning the Youth Council voted to integrate the city's downtown eating establishments. The experience of being served was fresh in their minds."[30]

The group first tried negotiation, opening up unpublicized talks with local merchants in May 1957. While these negotiations went on, they trained. For eighteen months the young people gathered together and studied nonviolent protest methods and theory. Meetings were held with black community leaders and with the children's parents. Finally, when the young people were ready, and after negotiations had failed, on August 18, 1958, thirteen youths and Clara Luper walked into Oklahoma City's Katz Drugstore and sat down at the soda fountain. Barbara Posey put a five-dollar bill on the counter and said, "We'd like thirteen Cokes, please." The civil rights movement's first lunch counter sit-in had begun.[31]

The first day the group was not served. "We decided to leave without cracking a dent in the wall," Luper writes. They returned on the next day and on succeeding days. Finally, on August 21, they were served. A day later they went to Kress's lunch counter, where they were served but had to stand because management had removed all the counter stools.

Graves notes wryly that the incident bore a striking resemblance to what southern newspaperman Harry Golden called the phenomenon of the "vertical Negro." In 1958, Golden noted that "vertical segregation" had been almost eliminated, as blacks and whites stood in the same grocery and department store lines. Problems arose, he noted, only when blacks sat down next to whites. He jokingly suggested that the solution was to remove the seats. Little did he know that someone would actually try such a thing.[32]

The sit-ins would continue at various locations until July 1964. During much of that time, until his appointment to the bench, Luther Bohanon viewed the burgeoning Oklahoma civil rights movement, as he viewed the national movement as a whole, with a sort of detached interest. While not opposed to it, he said, he was simply too busy practicing law to take much notice. Meanwhile, as the demonstrations continued, the NAACP again turned its attention to education. This return to school segregation as a target would soon cause Bohanon to take very great notice.[33]

In 1959, Dr. A. L. Dowell moved to 2700 North Bryant, across the street from the Oklahoma City School District, and enrolled his son Robert in school in the Pleasant Hill School District, an integrated independent school district northwest of Oklahoma City held out as a model of what integration could achieve.[34] Because Pleasant Hill provided classes only through grade nine, when Robert entered high school he was transferred to Frederick Douglass High School, a totally segregated facility in the Oklahoma City School District. The following year, Dr. Dowell requested that Robert be allowed to attend Northeast High

School, pointing out that numerous children from Pleasant Hill, both white and black, had been enrolled there the previous year.

When the request was denied as being "without merit," Dr. Dowell and his attorneys met with the school board. After lengthy discussions it was agreed that the boy could register at Northeast if he took a course in electronics unavailable at Douglass. When, however, Robert presented himself for enrollment at Northeast, Lederle J. Scott, the principal, "painted a very dark and doubtful picture to him" with regard to enrolling in the required electronics course, pointing out the "many hazards that might befall him should he undertake the course." Robert was clearly given the impression that "regardless of how hard he worked he would be met with reprisals to the extent that he should not undertake to enroll" at Northeast.[35] Instead he enrolled at Bishop McGuinness High School, an integrated Catholic school, and his father filed suit. They were represented by E. Melvin Porter, a local NAACP activist and later the first African-American to be elected to the state senate; John Green; and U. Simpson Tate, one of the team of attorneys that had successfully argued *Brown* in 1954.

Before filing the lawsuit, Dr. Dowell not only mapped out a strategy to attack the state's educational segregation laws, but he also prayed with his wife "for weeks on end." He and his Legal Defense Fund attorneys also caucused with local black leaders, including Clara Luper, who was Robert's advisor in the Youth Council and who would join in the case with her daughter as plaintiffs. "Many of my friends said I shouldn't rock the boat," he reported. "But, I felt on moral grounds that blacks should be able to attend any school they choose." In the end, Dowell came to a conclusion: "I figured the good Lord would probably take care of everything. But I wanted to help Him along."[36]

Although the case fell by lot to new judge Luther Bohanon, the complaint requested a three-judge panel, a technique used by civil rights attorneys previously with great success.[37] A panel was convened by the chief judge of the Tenth Circuit Court of Appeals, A. P. Murrah, Bohanon's former law partner. The panel consisted of Murrah, Bohanon, and Fred Daugherty, another district judge in Oklahoma. After a hearing on April 3, 1962, however, it was found that the issues raised were proper for adjudication and determination by a single judge, and the case was reassigned to Bohanon alone.

On July 11, 1963, a year and a half after the filing of Dowell's complaint, Bohanon issued his opinion (Dowell I), declaring the segregation provision of the Oklahoma State Constitution and the statutes enacted pursuant thereto unconstitutional and finding that the Oklahoma City School Board was enforcing a discriminatory system. He declared, "One of the basic foundations of America's strength, and one of the keys to its greatness, is the right to have equal public schools for all our children. The right of each American child to enjoy free equal schools. If any white child were denied such right all would be indignant; why not let it be so with our Negro children."[38]

He gave the school board ninety days to develop a comprehensive integration plan. Mindful of the loss of black teaching jobs in 1955 and believing that lack of black teachers and support personnel around them "to set an example to them of integration" would be a significant detriment to black children, Bohanon also became the first federal judge to order simultaneous integration of faculty and staff as well as students. In an interview, Bohanon stated that he was convinced of the need for such an order by Dr. E. C. Moon, local Oklahoma City dentist and a leader in the state's NAACP.[39]

The following morning, the *Daily Oklahoman* trumpeted, "Board to Appeal Race Case." Robert Dowell was quoted as saying, "I'm glad it's all over." An editorial entitled "Easier Said Than Done" discussed "white flight" and bussing (in an unfavorable light) and concluded that little more than token integration would occur because of segregated housing patterns.[40]

As ordered by Bohanon, the school board submitted a "Policy Statement Regarding Integration of the Oklahoma City Public Schools" in January 1964. The plan maintained the concept of neighborhood schools, assigning pupils to the schools in their zones without regard to race. Faculty and staff were also to be assigned without consideration of race. According to Bohanon, "the school board maintained that it had no affirmative duty to adopt policies that would result in integrated schools or destroy neighborhood schools."

Bohanon suggested that the board assemble an unbiased group to make an objective study of the problem and evaluate the plan. "When the school board balked at my suggestion, I took it as a lack of good faith on their part," writes Bohanon in his manuscript autobiography, "and directed that the plaintiffs gather the necessary information." A panel of three experts was assembled from throughout the nation and reported a year later.

The Spaulding Report, as it was known, found only slight improvement and token compliance on the part of Oklahoma City schools. The report recommended that a majority-to-minority transfer plan be put into effect and that two predominantly white junior high schools be paired with two predominantly black high schools. Faculty would, under the Spaulding proposal, be reassigned to reflect adjusted ethnic ratios in the schools.

After reading the Spaulding Report, writes Bohanon, "I failed to see how the action of the school board was in good faith. Instead, they were taking advantage of housing segregation to maintain school segregation." The judge therefore issued another opinion *(Dowell II)* in the school board case:

In this case Judge Bohanon extended those principles which he had begun to formulate in *Dowell I*. Not only did he reaffirm his displeasure with the Oklahoma City School Board for proceeding so slowly with integration, he took the first step toward forcing the board to comply with the *Brown* mandate. However harsh his treatment of the board might appear to be, in his opinion he had given them adequate time to comply with his order of July 11, 1963.

Bohanon stated, "Paper compliance and policy statements are insufficient to satisfy the standards of desegregation required by the second *Brown* decision."[41]

About the time that *Dowell II* was handed down, National Aeronautics and Space Administration (NASA) administrator James E. Webb, a Kerr protégé who had worked at Kerr-McGee in Oklahoma City before being appointed to the space agency, invited Judge Bohanon to accompany a group of prominent Oklahomans on a tour of NASA facilities throughout the country to see the program in operation.[42] By coincidence, on the first night of the trip, Bohanon was seated at dinner next to E. K. Gaylord, the powerful publisher of the *Daily Oklahoman* and *Oklahoma City Times*.

Edward King Gaylord had come to Oklahoma in 1903. By 1928 a local historian would describe him as "probably the most influential man in Oklahoma." He had been one of the leaders of the campaign for single statehood for the twin territories, and he led and won the fight to locate the state capital in Oklahoma City. He was called "an active factor in the state's every important movement." At the time of his encounter with Bohanon, he was at the height of his power. As publisher of the only two newspapers with statewide circulations and owner of WKY television and radio, he had a practical monopoly on opinion making within the state. He played an active role in state politics and his influence was felt in every development in Oklahoma government, business and finance.[43]

The pair seated together that first night were clearly at odds over the desegregation question and said nothing to each other through much of dinner. Finally, Gaylord turned to the judge and said, "I want you to know, Judge, that I am opposed to bussing of school children." Bohanon replied, "Editor, we've been bussing children for forty years." The publisher said nothing, and the two passed the remainder of the meal in silence.

Several nights later, at Cape Kennedy, the two were again seated next to one another. At length, Gaylord turned to Bohanon and said again, "I want you to know, Judge, that I am opposed to bussing of school children." Unfazed, Bohanon asked, "Well, editor, what are you going to do about the Constitution?" Once more Gaylord made no reply, and the pair never spoke again on the trip. From that time forward, however, the Gaylord media outlets were seldom favorable to Bohanon. Bohanon later recalled with a chuckle, "A word from the wise did not work."[44]

Illustrative of the antipathy between Bohanon and the Gaylord press, in a 1976 editorial the *Daily Oklahoman* lambasted the judge for suggesting that a hostile press had spurred on opposition to bussing in Oklahoma City (a charge to which it was arguably open), saying, "The rectitude of press support for equal education and integration of the public schools is undeniable ... and a matter of public record as well as public memory." Nine months later, in a similar opinion piece, the paper called Bohanon "imperial" and again self-servingly justified its own coverage, stating that it was not the press's role to "support" judges in their actions.[45]

Bohanon was "gratified" when *Dowell II* was narrowly upheld by the Tenth Circuit Court on January 23, 1967. Shortly thereafter, the Supreme Court denied certiorari and declined to hear further appeals.

While the litigation surrounding *Dowell II* proceeded, the school board, unknown to the judge, appointed a committee of fifty business and civic leaders to recommend ways to achieve integration in the schools. After many hours and thirty-five to forty meetings, the group, headed by Willis Wheat, developed a program. The Wheat Report called for transfers of students from neighborhood schools to achieve racial balance. Unfortunately, before the plan could be acted upon, it was leaked that the proposal called for bussing into predominantly black Harding Junior High and Northeast High to prevent them from reverting to all-black institutions as a result of white flight. When the school board met to consider the proposal, they were met by six hundred protestors. The board rejected the plan.[46]

At the same time the Wheat plan was being developed, the school board appointed a Committee on

Equality of Educational Opportunity (CEEO) to pre-
pare a plan. When the CEEO plan was delivered, it
called for a strict maintenance of neighborhood
schools. Special consideration would be given, however, to requests of minority students for transfer to
majority-dominated schools to achieve integration.
The board adopted the CEEO plan at an unannounced
meeting on May 30, 1969. Bohanon set both the Wheat
and CEEO plans for hearing on July 28, 1969.

At the outset of the hearing, Bohanon advised those
in attendance that the CEEO plan was rejected as not
being in good faith. Willis Wheat then testified, and arguments were heard from attorneys. At the conclusion
of the hearing, Judge Bohanon read to the school board,
which was seated in the jury box, the Supreme Court's
Brown II decision, explaining that it was the board's
duty to end segregation in the Oklahoma City public
schools. He then instructed them to present a plan in
keeping with the original request they had made to the
Wheat Committee. "The responsibility to formulate a
plan is on the school board," he said, "This court has
no right to try to run the school board."[47]

Dr. Virgil Hill, the president of the school board, said
that the board would develop a plan for presentation
two days later on July 30. He requested, however, that
the board be permitted to meet in closed session the
following day so that it could "deliberate without pressure." Bohanon agreed and ordered three U.S. marshals
to bar anyone but board members and the press from
attending. Given the short time frame set by Hill and
the request for a meeting in private, it seemed clear
that he had determined to adopt the Wheat plan.

The board met, however, without reaching a decision. Instead, they sent a request to Bohanon, asking
that he advise the board concerning the ratios of black

students to white students that should be maintained in each of the public schools. Bohanon refused, and the board met again on July 30. By a vote of three to two, they adopted the Wheat plan. On August 1, Bohanon ordered the Wheat plan implemented and charged the board to file a "full, comprehensive plan for complete desegregation and integration of the Oklahoma City Public School System as to students, faculty and employees of all grades" by November 1.[48]

As soon as Bohanon approved the Wheat plan, a citizens' group that had intervened in the proceedings appealed to the Tenth Circuit Court of Appeals, claiming that the plan violated the Civil Rights Act of 1964 by discriminating against white students. On August 5, the court of appeals vacated Bohanon's order approving the plan and remanded it to him for further consideration.

Bohanon was "incensed, embarrassed and humiliated." A week later, he took an action unprecedented in the history of the federal judiciary. He disobeyed the direction of the appellate court and for a second time ordered the Wheat plan implemented.

It was a tense summer, with confusion at the school board about what plan to follow, delays at the Tenth Circuit, and mixups with the mail and telephone calls from the Denver court. All the while, Oklahoma City's papers ran editorials fanning the flames.

The intervenors again appealed, this time joined by the school board, which reversed its previous decision and requested approval of the CEEO plan. The court of appeals, angered by the district judge's open defiance, again reversed Bohanon. This time, however, NAACP attorneys acted.

The Supreme Court was, at the time, in recess. At

such times, any single justice may act on behalf of the Court. Normally, urgent appeals such as that of the LDF would be heard by the justice with supervisory oversight of the specific appellate court from which the appeal came, in this case the Tenth Circuit Court. Ironically, this justice was Byron White, who, as assistant attorney general, had attempted to dissuade Senator Kerr from recommending Bohanon for the judiciary. White, however, was out of the country and unreachable. Instead, NAACP lawyer John Walker flew to Washington and appealed to Justice William Brennan, convincing him that the Tenth Circuit's ruling was in error. On August 29, Brennan overturned the appellate court's directive and reinstated Bohanon's original order. The opening of school was only four days away when he acted, and school board officials still professed a quandary over which plan to implement. In the end, they opted to obey Brennan and Bohanon's order. When the full Supreme Court reconvened in the fall, it upheld Brennan's decision.[49]

The day after Brennan's ruling, Chief Judge Murrah of the Tenth Circuit, who had issued the two orders vacating the Wheat plan, sent a note to his former law partner. It read tersely, "Dear Judge: You were right and we were wrong—may justice always prevail." The closing of the typewritten note, "with great respect," was followed by an illegible scrawl of a signature. Murrah then disqualified himself from continued participation in the school board case. He did so based on the fact that he had been a member of the original three-judge court that heard the case. The action was all the more odd in that it was more than seven years since that first hearing had taken place and the chief judge had seen no necessity to recuse himself previously. For

Bohanon, the incident had been so deeply insulting and embarrassing that it ruptured his relationship with his old friend and colleague forever.[50]

In Oklahoma City, protests against integration continued. On August 14, Bohanon was hanged in effigy from a street overpass. Angry citizens picketed, displaying placards which called him everything from a dictator and a Nazi to a Communist. Bumper stickers reading "Bus Bohanon" sprouted on car bumpers. Death threats and harassing phone calls and letters were received at his home. The FBI was called in to protect Mrs. Bohanon. When one mother defied the court's rulings and sent her fourteen-year-old son to his old school, Bohanon ordered the boy placed in the custody of a federal marshal. "It was shameful," Bohanon later said in an interview, "but you either have the courage or you don't. If it had been my brother, it would have been the same thing."[51]

On November 5, 1969, the school board adopted the "Comprehensive Plan for Complete Desegregation of Junior and Senior High Schools of the Oklahoma City Public Schools." Commonly called the Cluster Plan, the plan was an innovative proposal which viewed all schools as a unitary system and combined a variety of approaches: neighborhood schools, specialized facilities, an educational park, and modular scheduling.[52] Bohanon approved this "new concept in school utilization" in *Dowell III* on January 17, 1970.

The approval of the Cluster Plan further infuriated the populace. The right-wing American Party, founded in 1968 to advance George Wallace's bid for the presidency, called for Bohanon's impeachment for "abusive misuse of public authority." It described Bohanon's rulings as "un-American, conforming to the pattern of judges under Nazi, facist, and Soviet-type dictatorships." Three antibussing bills were introduced in the Oklahoma House of Representatives, and Altus representative Larry Derryberry set out to synthesize them into a single act that would withstand judicial scrutiny.[53]

With the failure of appeals over *Dowell III*, however, most of the issues in the Oklahoma City case were settled. The school board told Bohanon that "they would have an easier time in desegregating the schools if I would relinquish control of the process." Seeing this as an opportunity for the board to prove its good faith, Bohanon agreed to a "cooling off period" on August 21, 1970.

"Unfortunately," Bohanon writes, "in less than a year, on May 3, 1971, I was forced to reopen the case in response to a claim by Dowell's attorneys that the school board had failed to achieve a unitary system." In reviewing the facts, it became apparent to Bohanon that, left to its own devices, the school board had abandoned the Cluster Plan and had reverted to the CEEO plan. One of the authors of the plan, Raymond P. Lutz, an engineering professor at the University of Oklahoma, agreed. He stated that he was "disheartened when the school administration followed neither the principle of the plan as it was presented nor my later recommendations as to its implementation.[54]

Three proposals were submitted to the judge for consideration: the Cluster Plan, which the school board no longer supported, the Eibling plan, prepared by the school board and essentially a rehash of the CEEO plan, and a plan formulated by the plaintiffs, the Finger plan. The Finger plan, prepared by John Finger, a professor of education at Rhode Island State University who had previously worked with the Charlotte-Mecklenburg School System in its integration efforts, used to full advantage the Supreme Court's recent decision in *Swann* v. *Charlotte-Mecklenburg Board of Education* which permitted bussing and recognized the broad, equitable powers of federal judges to redress racial imbalance.

As the 1971–72 school year began, tensions were high. A new, more militant voice from the civil rights movement was inserting itself into the debate in Oklahoma City. On November 8, 1971, an unofficial Black Board of Education met to discuss the three proposals. Rev. Goree James, pastor of Saint John's Christian Methodist Episcopal Church, with the approval of the audience said that African-Americans must question whether "we are still as enthused, as excited as we were in 1956 about mixing." He said, "We admit defeat when we say that to have quality education we have to have white teachers and white students. I'm not a separatist, but let's not sell ourselves out. Everytime [*sic*] we break up anything black, we lose power."[55]

Concern was expressed at the meeting about allocation of federal funds. The unofficial board's president summed up the group's position: "We have to go where the whites are to get a half-way quality education, and that is where we're stuck, because the whites control the money."[56]

According to chroniclers of the *Dowell* case, "The *Swann* case had laid the groundwork for complete desegregation of the Oklahoma City school system." The Finger plan was the most comprehensive bussing scheme ever approved by a federal court to that time. On February 1, 1972, Judge Bohanon vacated the Cluster Plan and ordered implementation of the Finger plan *(Dowell IV)*. He wrote that "we have a plan that does not work, a plan that will not work, and a plan that will work." In such circumstances, the court had no other choice but to order implementation of the plan with the promise of working.[57]

Although Bohanon is quick to point out that "I did not order the bussing of a single child," he did authorize bussing as a legitimate means of achieving integregation. As he states, he "pointed out that bussing of school children was neither new nor novel and that bus transportation as a means to eliminate segregation may be validly employed." While the *Dowell* case has dragged on for another twenty years, it seemed in 1972 as though the Finger plan would pave the way for an end to segregation in the Oklahoma City schools.

Looking back, Bohanon admitted that he underestimated resistance to desegregation. "When [the *Dowell* case] was first filed, I felt that when people really understood what the law is, they would follow the law." There was no doubt in his mind what the Supreme Court had said in *Brown* and its progeny: "It's clear as a train-whistle—desegregate. I don't know of anything else I could have done different and lived with my conscience." Dr. A. L. Dowell agreed. In a 1981 interview, he said, "Busing has been a necessary evil. It has purged Oklahoma City of many of its hypocrises, its sins."[58]

In his 1972 decision, Bohanon also created a twelve-member Bi-Racial Committee, composed equally of whites and African-Americans. He charged the committee with the job of preparing recommendations to the school board on how best to achieve a unitary school system. He specifically cautioned, however, that the committee was not to supersede the board.

Nine days after Bohanon handed down *Dowell IV*, the school board filed a notice of appeal to his order to implement the Finger plan and to create the Bi-Racial

Committee. This time the Tenth Circuit refused to set aside Bohanon's order, "supported my actions, and affirmed the Finger plan and the Bi-Racial Committee." On subsequent petition, the Supreme Court again denied certiorari.

The last week of August 1972, the Oklahoma City public schools opened under the Finger plan. Opponents of bussing boycotted them. On Friday, September 1, at the start of the Labor Day weekend, an antibussing rally was held at which white hoods and Confederate flags were very much in evidence. The following day, at a press conference, Oklahoma City ministers called for "reconciliation and healing." Rev. Henry Roerson of Sacred Heart Catholic Church had called the group of eight clergy, representing Lutheran, Presbyterian, United Methodist, and Catholic churches, together because he was concerned about the "violent, hate-filled situation that exists." A prepared statement called for parents and children to create a situation in which "existing laws (which currently call for carrying out of the Finger Plan) will be enforced and implemented."

The same day, Rev. Goree James, speaking on behalf of an ad hoc human relations council, called for a Labor Day meeting of clergy at Trinity Presbyterian Church to find some way "to defuse the volatile situation surrounding the opening of school under the Finger Plan. He openly appealed for antibussing leaders to join him "in asking for calm and reconciliation" and went on to say that he prayed that both blacks and whites would "fail to listen to unproven leaders who cannot deliver what they promise. . . . I am encouraged and feel that there is more good will in every section of our city than there is hate." James stated that he felt bussing opponents "can join with us in peace and love as Jesus taught us, without breaching their principles on bussing."[59]

State NAACP president Wade Watts, a Baptist minister from McAlester, announced that he would travel to Oklahoma City. Bohanon was again hanged in effigy, this time by Oklahoma City students.[60] On Sunday, cars sporting American and Confederate flags paraded in Oklahoma City.

When schools reopened on Tuesday, approximately twenty-six ministers led by James and some concerned citizens, including members of the Optimist Club, turned out at Southeast and Capitol Hill high schools. James stressed that the groups were not there "to take over the schools. We're here to keep the peace and to cooperate with whoever else is here." The only incidents were a few cars of youths driving around Capitol Hill and U.S. Grant high schools, honking, and, once again, flying Confederate flags.[61]

In this highly charged atmosphere, the Bi-Racial Committee began its work, focusing on the integration of the school system's administrative personnel and faculties. Among other suggestions, the committee recommended that the African-American principal of Frederick Douglass High School be reassigned to John Marshall High School and that John Marshall's white principal be sent to Douglass. They also suggested that the black principal of Northeast High School and the white chief administrator of U.S. Grant High School be exchanged. These and other recommendations were part of an effort to racially balance the system's faculties. When the school board rejected the committee's work, Bohanon ordered the recommendations implemented.

Judge Bohanon recalled, "Although the school board appealed to the Tenth Circuit Court, my decision was upheld." In his autobiography, he writes somewhat optimistically, "With its legal options at an end, the school board accepted the complete integration of the school system and administrative personnel."

Bohanon expressed satisfaction at the work of the Bi-Racial Committee. The school board continued over the ensuing months to wrangle in the courts but got nowhere. Gradually it settled into operation of the Finger plan. Tragic incidents continued, however, to mar the integration process. When racial violence broke out in 1975, a white student was killed. Judge Bohanon received a letter, containing only a newspaper article on the slaying. Across the top, the sender had printed in pencil, "Bohannon [sic]: 1, Christians: 0."[62]

That same year, after only three years of operations under the Finger plan, the school board filed a motion to close the case, arguing that it had "eliminated all vestiges of state imposed racial discrimination in its school system." After an evidentiary hearing on January 19, 1977, Bohanon, believing that the board was in good-faith compliance with his previous orders, granted the motion and issued an order terminating the case. He concluded that the Oklahoma City School Board had operated the Finger plan properly, that the plan and the Bi-Racial Committee had been effective, and that "substantial compliance with the constitutional requirements" had been achieved. In the order, he stated that he did not "foresee that the termination of . . . jurisdiction will result in the dismantlement of the Plan or any affirmative action by the defendant to undermine the unitary system so slowly and painfully accomplished over the 16 years during which the cause has been pending before the Court.[63]

The following evening, Gaylord's *Oklahoma City Times* again criticized Judge Bohanon for his previous rulings. The school board upon which he had repeatedly "come down hard" had only, the paper argued, been representing the majority of Oklahoma Cityans who favored neighborhood schools. It went on to caution those who welcomed the end of court supervision that the city might be in for something far worse, as its schools now became "subject to the whims of the zealots in the Office of Civil Rights of the U.S. Department of Health, Education and Welfare."[64]

While the terminating order ended the district court's active, day-to-day supervision of the school board, it did not dissolve the injunctive decree under which the board was operating. The plaintiffs did not appeal. Years later, Bohanon would reflect, "I was of the firm belief and conviction that my order of January 19 terminating Federal Court supervision of the school board, which was based upon the creation of a unitary school district, freed the school board to take any action within its jurisdiction until a showing that the school board had willfully and intentionally discriminated against black students."

For almost nine years, without supervision by Bohanon's court, the Oklahoma City School Board continued to operate under the Finger plan. Bohanon felt confident that the board was "now sensitized to the constitutional implications of its conduct and with a new awareness of its responsibility to citizens of all races."[65] Then in 1984, the board adopted the Student Reassignment Plan (SRP).

The school board claimed that "substantial demographic changes in Oklahoma City had rendered parts of the Finger Plan inequitable and oppressive and thus because of these changes they prepared a modification of the original plan." The SRP superimposed attendance zones over some racially segregated areas. It also eliminated compulsory bussing and assigned pupils to neighborhood schools from kindergarten through the fourth grade. The scheme was to take effect in September 1985.[66]

In response to the SRP, Dowell's attorneys moved to reopen the case before Bohanon, challenging the school board's decision to alter the basic method of pupil assignment at the elementary school level. While some Oklahoma City blacks were willing to give neighborhood schools a chance, others, including plaintiff Clara Luper, were not. Luper declared, "Maybe I'm old-fashioned, but I still believe it's better for blacks and whites to be in the same classroom— better to learn about each other firsthand.... When you wait until a child is in the fifth grade until he or she has any contact with other races, that child is scarred forever."[67]

Bohanon found that "as a result of the new plan some schools became predominantly black." In fact, as Justice Thurgood Marshall later noted, "As a result, considerable racial imbalance reemerged in 33 of 64 elementary schools in the Oklahoma City system with student bodies either greater than 90% Afro-American or greater than 90% non–Afro-American. More specifically, 11 of the schools ranged from 96.9% to 99.7% Afro-American, and approximately 44% of all Afro-American children in grades K–4 were assigned to these virtually all–Afro-American schools." These virtually all-black schools were "the same all-black schools that had been sanctioned by state law during the days of Jim Crow." The figures are all the more startling when one considers that the operation of the Finger plan had completely eliminated all-black schools.[68]

These facts alone, however, Bohanon believed, did

not require a finding of unconstitutionality. He based his belief on two relatively recent Supreme Court opinions, *Swann* v. *Charlotte-Mecklenburg Board of Education* (the same case that he had used to support his initial decree ordering implementation of the Finger plan) and *Keyes* v. *School District No. 1*. In *Swann*, the Court recognized that few communities served by school districts with newly acquired unitary status would remain demographically stable. In *Keyes*, the justices also stated that "at some point in time the relationship between past segregation acts and present segregation may become so attentuated as to be incapable of de jure segregation warranting judicial intervention." Further, in *Swann* the Court explicitly stated:

Neither school authorities nor district courts are constitutionally required to make year-to-year adjustments of the racial composition of students bodies once the affirmative duty to desegregate has been accomplished and racial discrimination through official action is eliminated from the system. This does not mean that federal courts are without power to deal with future problems; but in the absence of a showing that either the school authorities or some other agency of the State has deliberately attempted to fix or alter demographic patterns to affect the racial composition of schools, further intervention by a district court should not be necessary.[69]

Following an evidentiary hearing in April 1985, Bohanon found that the unitary status of the school system in 1977 still prevailed. He concluded that the neighborhood school plan was constitutional "because it was not adopted with the intent to discriminate on the basis of race." He had surrendered his supervision of the school board as mandated by the Supreme Court

in the *Swann* case, and he did not find the special circumstances necessary to warrant reopening the matter. He thus denied the plaintiffs' request.

On appeal, the plaintiffs objected to the ruling, con-
tending that had Bohanon reopened the case they
would have introduced new evidence. Bohanon's pride
and impassive devotion to the edicts of the Supreme
Court, which had so often benefited the civil rights activists, now began to cut the other way. He termed this
contention of the plaintiffs "ridiculous."

Bohanon contends that in 1977 with his order of termination he had intended fully "to restore the Oklahoma City School system to total independence and
relinquish to the board all control over the school district." In 1986, however, the Tenth Circuit Court of
Appeals, in a highly technical opinion, ruled that only
when an order terminating a case also dissolved the desegregation decree did a school board gain full independence from the previous injunction. Because Judge
Bohanon had not dissolved the district court's 1972 order, the appellate court remanded the case to him to
determine whether the original mandatory order
should be enforced, modified, or terminated.

Bohanon termed the Tenth Circuit's 1986 decision,
remanding *Dowell* to him for further proceedings, "the
most shocking order I had ever received from an appellate court." Years later, he would write, "There can be
no question that the order remanding for rehearing was
in error and without merit. It was devastating to the
Oklahoma City School Board and a revolting situation
for the district court. In all my judicial work, I have
never been so upset and saddened as I was with the circuit court's order of June 6, 1986."

Judge Bohanon's memoirs reflect a distinct lack of

enthusiasm for again revisiting the situation of which he had tried to be rid twice before. He wrote, "Like a good soldier, however, I followed the order."

On February 5, 1987, he granted Dowell's lawyers motion to reopen the suit and set the matter down for a hearing on the merits of the case. After eight days of testimony in June, Bohanon once again carefully reviewed all evidence and the transcript of the hearing. Once more, he found the Oklahoma City system to be in compliance and declared the SRP to be constitutional. In a pointed reference to his disagreement with the appellate court, he wrote, "The court again, as in 1977, terminates its jurisdiction over this unitary system."[70]

Although Dowell's attorneys once more appealed to the court of appeals in Denver, Bohanon expressed confidence that this decision would be affirmed. On July 7, 1989, however, in a curt opinion, the court again reversed, finding that the school board had failed to meet its burden of establishing that the condition the decree "sought to alleviate, a constitutional violation, has been eradicated."[71]

The appellate tribunal stated that "an injunction takes on a life of its own and becomes an edict quite independent of the law it is meant to effectuate." A desegregation decree thus, according to the court, remains in effect until a school district can show "grievous wrong evoked by new and unforeseen conditions"—"dramatic changes in conditions unforeseen at the time of the decree that . . . impose extreme and unexpectedly oppressive hardships on the obligor." The school board had not met that test. Given that, as previously noted, the SRP would result in a number of schools' returning to single-race institutions, the court held that the board had an "affirmative duty . . . not to take any action that would impede the process of disestablishing the dual system and its effects."[72]

A few days after the circuit court's ruling, Judge Bohanon was hospitalized, suffering from chest pains, and he underwent heart bypass surgery shortly thereafter. As is seen repeatedly throughout his career, Bohanon, like most other trial court judges, has demonstrated a marked aversion to being reversed. Given therefore the timing of the illness, one can only speculate about the effect of the 1989 reversal upon the eighty-six-year-old jurist.

The school board again appealed to the U.S. Supreme Court. This time the high court granted its petition for certiorari. The case was argued on October 2, 1990, and a decision was handed down on January 15 of the following year. In a 5–3 decision the Court found for the school board. Justice David Souter, having been appointed and confirmed only recently, was not on the Court at the time the case was argued. He therefore took no part in the decision.

Writing for the majority, Chief Justice William Rehnquist declared that the court in Denver had held the school board to too stringent a standard. He stated, "The test espoused by the Court of Appeals would condemn a school district, once governed by a board which intentionally discriminated, to judicial tutelage for the indefinite future." He thus rejected the contention of Dowell lawyer Julius Chambers, the director of the NAACP Legal Defense and Education Fund, that the injunction implied essentially permanent supervision of schools. When asked in an interview how long an injunction ought to remain in place, Chambers replied, "I'd ask, 'How long will discrimination last?' "[73]

The case was once more remanded to Judge Bohanon's court for further determinations. In examining the case again, he was instructed to determine whether the board had complied in good faith with his order from the time it was entered in 1972 and whether, in light of every facet of school operations, student assignments, faculty, staff, transportation, extracurricular activities, and facilities, "the vestiges of *de jure* segregation had been eliminated as far as practicable." In so doing, the Court cautioned, the "district court need not accept at face value the profession of a school board which has intentionally discriminated that it will cease to do so in the future." It also stated that, after deciding, according to the criteria it had set forth, whether the school board was entitled to have the decree terminated, Bohanon was also to examine the SRP by itself to determine whether it met the requirements of the Constitution. Rehnquist wrote, "A school district which has been released from an injunction imposing a desegregation plan no longer requires court authorization for the promulgation of policies and rules regulating matters such as assignment of students and the like, but it of course remains subject to the mandate of the Equal Protection Clause of the Fourteenth Amendment."[74]

Justice Marshall, one of the team of attorneys who argued *Brown* before the Court in 1954, wrote a lengthy and detailed dissent. Joined by Justices Blackmun and Stevens, he reviewed the long history of segregation in Oklahoma. Marshall conceded that in *Brown* and its successors the Supreme Court had never contemplated perpetual oversight of school systems, but, he implied, in the case of the Oklahoma City school system it was too soon to declare victory and vacate the battlefield. Federal courts should never be induced "to renounce supervision of unfinished tasks

because of the lateness of the hour." The dissent argued that even if there was no evidence of unremoved
vestiges of *de jure* segregation, Bohanon should antici-
pate what effect the lifting of the decree would have in
order to adequately assess the case for its dissolution.[75]

The dissenters focused on the stigmatic injury to
African-American children done by segregation. The
dissent quoted *Brown I:* "To separate them from
others of similar age and qualifications solely because
of their race generates a feeling of inferiority as to their
status in the community that may affect their hearts
and minds in a way very unlikely ever to be undone."
Such stigmatic harm can persist even after the state
ceases to enforce segregation. It concluded, "In a
district with a history of state-sponsored school segregation, racial separation ... *remains* inherently unequal."[76]

Reaction to the Supreme Court decision was predictably mixed. School board president Thelma Parks
expressed relief, stating that the Tenth Circuit's guidelines "would have kept school districts such as ours
under federal court order until the end of time." U.S.
Solicitor General Kenneth Starr called the opinion
"the first important school case in 10 years" and said,
"The court made it crystal clear that federal supervision of a school system is a temporary state. It has a
beginning, but it also must have a conclusion." An
editorial in the *Daily Oklahoman,* entitled "Forced
Busing: A Beginning and End," said that "it seems
clear there's a light at the end of the tunnel." And the
Wall Street Journal stated that although the majority
opinion did not "openly retreat" from the principles of
Brown, "it signaled that the era of continuous federal
court scrutiny of school desegregation plans may be
drawing to a close."[77]

Civil rights advocates were more cautious. One merely noted with grim irony that the high court had seen fit to issue its opinion on the birthday of Martin Luther King. Janell Byrd, one of Dowell's lawyers from the Legal Defense Fund, said that it was not "a full retreat" from *Brown* and agreed with Julius Chambers: "The arsenal of desegregation holdings remains intact." Former LDF chief counsel Jack Greenberg disagreed, saying it was clearly a retreat. He stated that opinions like "*Swann* and *Dowell* legitimize the way of thinking which says eventually every place is going to be like Montreal or Calgary or Reykjavik, and courts won't come in to clean it up. Of course, that's not possible in a southern community with a history of discrimination." Both the American Civil Liberties Union and the National Education Association said that the case was not definitive. Byrd said the case was troubling nonetheless because they felt that they had already met the test set down by the Court, in clearly showing "that vestiges of segregation have not been eliminated in Oklahoma City."[78]

Nevertheless, the case that Luther Bohanon tried three times to conclude was once more before his court. The Supreme Court had ordered him to review anew all aspects of the case. In particular, they instructed him to treat the question of residential segregation as *res nova,* a new thing.[79]

Between 1972 and 1985, the period during which the school board operated under the Finger plan ordered by Judge Bohanon, the test scores of African-American children in Oklahoma City increased. Such children benefited from increased funding of previously all-black schools. According to Lettie Ruth Hunter, a teacher and a member of the Equity Committee, a successor to the Bi-Racial Committee, "When we had white kids bused in here, all of a sudden we got some money to fix things up." African-American students also gained access to schools with better resources in the city's more affluent neighborhoods. Hunter went on: "At least our children could take advantage of computers and better facilities. I don't think that would have happened without integration." Today, however, according to Dowell's lawyers, with the re-emergence of single-race schools, test scores are again in decline and funding disparities jeopardize hard-won gains.[80]

W. B. Parker, a minister and member of the Equity Committee, recalled the days of Jim Crow, saying, "Wasn't a white face in our classroom. . . . We couldn't get enough books, enough supplies. We couldn't even get our buildings heated. . . . Today I walk through some of these schools in the black neighborhoods, and *nothing's* changed. They're as run-down as ever, the paint's peeling, and some teachers have to buy books for the kids. . . . And you don't see a white child anywhere."[81]

Professor Andrew Hacker reported in a recent book that of the thirty-two states containing 98.2 percent of the United States' African-American population, Oklahoma ranked only twenty-sixth in segregation, with just over 40 percent of its black student population attending racially unmixed schools.[82] This somewhat encouraging, though still wholly unacceptable, statistic, however, masks a much grimmer reality. In Tulsa and Oklahoma City, where most of the state's blacks reside, the percentage attending single-race institutions would be much higher.

Despite this state of affairs, Judge Bohanon was clearly in no mood to have the case back before him. Frustrated by his inability to make his rulings stick and stung by what he considered a personal affront in reversals by higher courts, Bohanon dug in his heels, ever increasingly convinced in his own mind of the school board's compliance with constitutional standards. In October 1991 he denied an LDF motion to hold an evidentiary hearing. He did, however, schedule oral arguments for the following November 18. But twelve days before that scheduled appearance he abruptly canceled the court date. The following day, he handed down a voluminous opinion which stated that there was no need for further hearings or submissions of evidence. Bohanon wrote bitingly, "The Supreme Court's instructions do not order this court to 'conduct' further proceedings; nor did the Supreme Court use any other language indicating that further hearings should be pursued." He ruled that because the court was to decide if the school board was entitled to have the injunction dissolved as of 1985, nothing after the 1987 hearing was relevant. The parties had submitted a "golconda" of evidence at that time. The record was complete.[83]

The opinion, 112 pages long, was almost identical to the proposed ruling contained in a brief filed by the school board the previous May, and it found for the defendant board on all points, dissolving the injunction "totally and completely."[84] In his conclusion, Judge Bohanon wrote somewhat myopically:

The long history of this case demonstrates the federal courts' proper sensitivity to the need to protect the civil rights of every child in this land. This court will remain ever vigilant in the protection of those rights. The background of this case reflects the great progress that has been made over the years in the vindication of these rights for the black children of Oklahoma City, from the repeal of palpably unconstitutional and disgraceful legal mandates and official policies, to the enactment of new legal protections, and the long, arduous, step-by-step dismantling of the dual school system. It is time to recognize that progress. While the history of discrimination in Oklahoma City cannot be ignored, it "cannot, in the manner of original sin, condemn governmental action that is not itself unlawful."[85]

Oklahoma City school superintendent Arthur Steller hailed the decision. At a press conference following the issuance of the opinion, he declared, "What this does is makes us feel vindicated from all the discrimination claims people have made. This is yet another indication that this district is not a district that discriminates."[86]

Civil rights activists were blunt. LDF's Janell Byrd stated that the decision was an event "of very destructive and tragic proportions for not only the school children in the Oklahoma City school district, but also for race relations in Oklahoma City." Local NAACP president Roosevelt Milton said that the ruling didn't surprise him, especially "given today's climate in which David Duke can run for governor of Louisiana and nobody is ashamed of this happening."[87]

Less than thirty days after the ruling, Dowell's attorneys filed a motion for relief from the court's judgment. In their application they claimed that events subsequent to the 1987 hearing raised "very serious questions as to the continuing accuracy of the conclusions supporting" the trial court's opinion. These developments, they argued, demonstrated "the inequity of adhering to a judgment that prematurely cut" the plaintiffs off from full relief for the harm caused by the school board's long-standing operation of a racially segregated and discriminatory system.[88]

Judge Bohanon had had enough. The motion ran counter to his explicit instruction directing the court clerk not to accept any further applications to reopen the case without the judge's prior approval. Even though the school board had not objected to the motion, Bohanon rejected it on January 2, 1992, finding it to be "wholly without merit." He flatly told them that they were free to appeal his November 7 opinion and judgment.[89]

It was a far cry from fifteen years before, when Dowell's lawyers had moved for the award of attorneys' fees. In granting that motion, Judge Bohanon wrote:

Spurred by a press hostile to the constitutional concept of equal education for all children, the Board has pursued a deliberate course of delay, obstruction and evasion in the implementation of a unitary system. By its obstinate disregard of its constitutional responsibilities, it compelled the plaintiffs to claim, demand, struggle for and defend that which was constitutionally theirs. Willing to spend and exhaust the resources of the school district in fruitless endeavors to frustrate plaintiffs' constitutional rights, the Board made necessary the very services by counsel for plaintiffs whose cost it now opposes. The Board is responsible for its betrayal of the trust imposed by citizens of the district. The consequences of its wanton stewardship must not be borne alone by the very parties whose rights were denied. Indeed the vindication of their rights under the Constitution is necessarily an affirmation of the rights of every citizen and of benefit to all who respect and cherish the values of our Constitution.[90]

The history of the *Dowell* case does indeed depict a "sad tale." In 1972, James Stewart stated that Oklahoma City blacks were "tired of hearing . . . the expression of some people that, 'We're sorry for the mistakes of the past, but it won't happen again.' History shows it does happen again."[91]

Although he denies it when directly confronted, as the *Dowell* case has been increasingly protracted, its estimation in Judge Bohanon's eyes has diminished. He now speaks with greater affection about the *Selected Investments* matter. Janell Byrd has announced the LDF's intention to appeal the November 7 decision, so Judge Bohanon may not yet have succeeded in dismissing the matter. Whatever happens, there is almost certain to be additional controversy for a man whose career has been filled with controversy. While he does not seek it out, "I'm getting used to it," he remarks with a sigh.[92]

In the mid-1970s, as the initial furor over implementation of the Finger plan was dying away, Bohanon became embroiled in another case wherein he would face similar public hostility and institutional indifference. The case involved Oklahoma's prisons and an inmate named Bobby Battle.

Chapter V

The Prison Case

*[A] policy of judicial restraint cannot encompass any fail-
ure to take cognizance of valid constitutional claims
whether arising in a federal or state institution. When a
prison regulation or practice offends a fundamental constitutional guarantee, federal courts will discharge their duty
to protect constitutional rights.*

JOHNSON V. AVERY,
393 U.S. 483 (1969)

*The Court has the authority and duty to insure that the
Constitution does not stop at the prison gate, but rather in-
ures to the benefit of all, even those citizens behind prison
walls.*

BATTLE V. ANDERSON,
447 F. Supp. 516 (E.D. Okl. 1977)

FEDERAL courts have been asked with increasing fre-
quency in recent years to issue injunctive decrees that
would restructure public institutions in accordance
with what are asserted to be the dictates of the
U.S. Constitution. These "institutional cases" seek to
bring into harmony with federal constitutional standards institutions as disparate as public schools and

117

mental hospitals, state militias and penitentiaries. The defendants in such cases are state officials, and the aim is to compel those officials to take such action as is necessary to bring the institutions for which they are responsible into line with constitutional norms.[1]

The institutional cases have been a source of controversy among legal scholars, governments, and the public at large. Opponents argue that separation of powers and principles of federalism should bar federal judges from interfering with the affairs and conduct of these state institutions. Proponents defend the decisions, pointing out that institutional decrees are not unprecedented: the old English writ of mandamus, which compelled action by a public officer, said little about why the King's Bench could do what it did beyond the bare statement that an injustice had been committed and had to be set right.[2]

Thirty years ago, as Theodore Eisenberg and Stephen Yeazell point out, few would have thought that the Constitution "guaranteed mental patients clean sheets or prisoners hearings before parole boards. Having found such rights implied by the Constitution, courts have reached for a remedial arsenal fitted out centuries ago for service in other wars. The weapons are not new, but the cause is, and one must finally evaluate such litigation in terms of its ends rather than means."[3] The end is to demonstrate, as Judge Bohanon wrote, that the Constitution does not stop "at the prison gate"—or the threshold of Bedlam, or the schoolhouse door.

During his tenure, Judge Bohanon has been called upon to adjudicate a number of institutional cases. In addition to *Dowell* and the prison case, *Battle* v. *Anderson,* he has also decided cases dealing with discrimination in Oklahoma's National Guard (*Thornton* v.

Coffey), housing discrimination (*Dailey* v. *City of Lawton* and *Anderson* v. *Forest Park*), the right to an education for the physically challenged (*Helms* v. *Independent School District No. 3 of Broken Arrow*), and unlawful sex discrimination arising from mandatory maternity leave policies (*Fabian* v. *Independent School District No. 89*).[4]

Illustrative of the acrimony these institutional cases generate is a November 6, 1981, editorial in Edward L. Gaylord's *Oklahoma City Times*. Reporting a speech by U.S. Attorney General William French Smith, the opinion piece, entitled "Judges Overstep Power," stated:

> The attorney general contended that "federal courts have gone far beyond their abilities" in imposing remedies for perceived constitutional violations. He cited decisions in school integration cases and in imposing racial or minority quotas in the workplace.
>
> He said that "federal courts have attempted to restructure entire school systems in desegregation cases—and to maintain continuing review over basic administrative decisions. They have asserted similar control over entire prison systems and public housing projects.
>
> "They have restructured the employment criteria to be used by American business and government—even to the extent of mandating numerical results based on race and gender. At least one federal judge had even attempted to administer a local sewer system."
>
> The attorney general contends the federal courts by overstepping their powers "have forced major reallocations of governmental resources—often with no concern for budgetary limits and the dislocations that inevitably result from limited judicial perspective."
>
> Oklahomans can vouch for the accuracy of that statement. While spending millions of dollars for new prison facilities under a court-ordered mandate to provide convicts

with more individual cell space, the rate of crime continues to increase.[5]

The article was a pointed barb at Luther Bohanon and his case *Battle* v. *Anderson.*

It is axiomatic among lawyers that the weakest link in any civil rights suit is usually the plaintiff. That is, those challenging deprivation of constitutionally protected rights are, by definition, those outside of the mainstream; often they are persons whom that mainstream would find personally and actively distasteful. This was certainly true in the case of *Battle* v. *Anderson.* Bobby Battle was an unlikely hero: an African-American inmate serving time for robbery at Oklahoma's maximum-security state penitentiary at McAlester.[6]

In 1970 the Oklahoma prison system was still, in many ways, in the Middle Ages. It was described by more than one knowledgeable person as one of the most "inefficient, archaic and corrupt" such systems in the country. The McAlester penitentiary, which was created by the state legislature at statehood, had become the stereotypical prison of 1930s motion pictures, "complete with unmerciful discipline, brutal guards, and a recidivism rate of 70%." "Big Mac," as it came to be called, was filled to 219 percent of designed capacity. Cells designed for one or two persons held three and four, and when that space was gone, prisoners were forced to sleep in libraries, garages, stairwells, and hallways. Sanitary facilities were often inoperative, and sewage backed up into cells. Mail was censored. Whites and African-Americans were segregated as a matter of official policy. Prisoners were subjected to food service that was described as "sickening." These problems were exacerbated by an incarceration rate that was twice the national average and a parole policy that kept inmates confined 50 percent longer than the national average.[7]

Battle was one of those who witnessed the abuses from the inside. In 1970, following a particularly senseless beating, hundreds of McAlester inmates refused to return to their cells and, led by Battle, staged a sit-down strike to protest the beating. For their actions, Battle and the other strikers were put in solitary confinement, the "hole," for ninety days. The hole was a totally dark, windowless cell equipped only with a toilet and a sink. In the aftermath of the strike, physical abuse by corrections officers grew worse. In an effort to redress their grievances, Battle and five other prisoners submitted a petition, citing specific objections, to prison officials. There was no action.

On April 24, 1972, Battle brought suit against Warden Park J. Anderson and the Oklahoma Department of Corrections. Represented by attorneys from the American Civil Liberties Union (ACLU), Battle alleged that the constitutional and civil rights of inmates were being violated by state officials who subjected them to cruel and unusual punishment and denied them the rights of due process; equal protection under the laws; freedom of speech, religion, and assembly; redress of grievances; and access to the courts. Through his lawyers, Battle specifically requested injunctive relief to end the abuses. Within a year, the Civil Rights Division of the U.S. Department of Justice intervened on behalf of the plaintiff inmates.

The Justice Department lawyers, in conjunction with their ACLU counterparts, began to take depositions at McAlester to get a clearer picture of conditions at the prison. What they found was profoundly shocking.

Inmate treatment had changed little in the almost seventy years since the prison was built. Total designed capacity at McAlester was 1,200. By 1972, however, the average inmate population was 1,778, with a racial mix of seventy percent white, Native American, and other minorities and thirty percent African-American. The inmates were segregated officially by race, with the best prison jobs going to nonblack prisoners.

To control the inmates, the prison employed only 242 security personnel. Most of these guards were inadequately trained and poorly supervised. Turnover of personnel averaged between 8 and 9 percent per month. Often only a single guard was on duty inside each cell house, with another two on patrol in the main yard. Because of these inadequacies, an alarming level of violence existed inside the penitentiary. Between January 1970 and the end of July 1973 there had been nineteen violent deaths, forty stabbings, and forty-four serious beatings inside the prison. Drug abuse, alcoholism, and loan sharking were pandemic.

In order to offset the insufficient number of guards, the prisoners were subjected to harsh discipline, which could take the form of isolation, withdrawal of privileges, tear gassing, or beatings. Some, but not all, infractions were printed in an inmate rule book. Other regulations were published only in employee manuals.

Only serious cases came before the formal disciplinary committee; however, inmates charged with serious infractions were placed immediately in the lockup area. Because the disciplinary committee generally met weekly, prisoners could spend as long as six days in the lockup before a hearing. There were no regular members of the disciplinary committee, and often inmates were judged by the same officers who brought the charges against them. Prisoners were allowed to be heard during the hearing but were denied counsel and the right to call witnesses or to cross-examine adverse witnesses.

The official in charge of the Maximum Security Unit was allowed to punish inmates summarily without a hearing. Sleeping accommodations in the Maximum Security Unit consisted of a mattress placed on the floor. Light was inadequate, and vermin infested the cells. It was common for prisoners to be held for prolonged periods in close confinement, with exercise periods limited to fifteen minutes twice a week. Inmates could be moved to an isolation cell within the Maximum Security Unit at the sole discretion of the official in charge. Inmates in the isolation cells were not permitted any exercise outside of their cells. In addition, those sentenced to seventy-two hours' "detention" were placed in the hole.

Medical facilities available at the main penitentiary were incapable of meeting even the routine health care needs of prisoners. Emergency services were unavailable. Because of the shortage of adequate personnel, untrained correctional officers were given responsibility for triage, screening inmates to determine who would be allowed to see the duty physician. They also treated minor wounds and injuries. Dental services were provided by a series of part-time dentists who did not have the capacity to provide long-term dental care. While fully half of the inmates at McAlester were in need of professional psychiatric care, none was available on a regular basis. Instead, a visiting psychiatrist made weekly visits. Psychiatric treatment usually consisted of nothing more than heavy sedation to control violent prisoners.

Before the ACLU's depositions could be completed, conditions at Big Mac reached the breaking point. At

2:20 P.M. on July 27, 1973, between twenty-five and thirty inmates seized guards in the mess hall and encouraged fellow convicts to riot. Within a short time, approximately six hundred prisoners were involved. Prison buildings were set on fire, the prison yard was in the hands of the rioters, and the situation was beyond the control of prison guards. At one point, an inmate announced over the public address system, "This is a revolution." Prison authorities ordered the lawyers involved in depositions to leave the prison.[8]

In answer to a plea for help, elements of the Oklahoma Highway Patrol and units of the Oklahoma Army and Air national guards were sent to the penitentiary to reinforce prison personnel. Four state officials—Chairman of the State Board of Corrections Irvine Ungerman, Director of the Department of Corrections Leo McCracken, Commissioner of Public Safety Wayne Lawson, and Warden Anderson—worked through the night to restore peace. Hostages were released at 11:30 A.M. the following day. Although the riot officially ended at noon on July 28, it took a massive show of force, including use of tear gas, and another seven days before all prisoners were again confined to their cells. The prison was little more than a smoldering ruin. Damages were estimated at twenty million dollars.[9] Four prisoners were dead, and forty others, both inmates and guards, were injured.

Judge Bohanon had inherited *Battle* v. *Anderson* from Judge Edwin Langley, chief judge of the Eastern District of Oklahoma, when Judge Langley suffered heart problems. Eight days after the riot ended, on August 12, 1973, Bohanon issued his first order in the case. By agreement among the attorneys, twenty depositions, containing over thirty thousand words of testimony, were admitted into evidence, and the matter was set for trial on March 14, 1974. In the meantime, discovery was to continue. Subsequently, in September, Judge Langley died, and the case fell permanently to Bohanon.

In the wake of the riot, treatment of prisoners at McAlester grew worse. Inmates were confined to their cells twenty-four hours a day in complete idleness. No exercise or recreation was permitted. Until April 1974, prisoners were allowed outside their cells only once or twice every other day to eat in the dining hall.

The *Battle* trial began as scheduled. The following day, on the afternoon of March 15, Bohanon announced his decision, in favor of the inmates, from the bench. Any hope that, after thirteen years on the bench and with the approach of his seventy-second birthday, Bohanon might have softened was dispelled by the ruling. His decision was a sweeping indictment of the prison at McAlester, finding that it failed to meet constitutional standards on any level. He stated, "Treatment is so shameful it is no wonder they commit the worst acts known to man." Calling the system "shameful and disgraceful," he declared, "I had no idea until this week of the deep cruelty inmates were subjected to." He enjoined prison officials from continuing a lengthy series of abuses and ordered them to correct a long list of deficiencies.[10]

As Bohanon finished reading his decision, tears welled in Bobby Battle's eyes. Then he smiled. As he was led from the courtroom by his guards, he raised a clenched fist in triumph.[11]

The decision was immediately hailed by ACLU attorney Mary Bane as "the most significant ruling of prison litigation in the United States." The judge's written opinion, filed with the court clerk six weeks later on May 30, would do nothing to diminish that estimation. The opinion ran sixty legal-sized pages and contained forty-three individual orders to the corrections officials. The opinion became a benchmark in institutional adjudication. Among other things, the decision was among the first to recognize the legitimacy of the Black Muslim faith.[12]

"Notwithstanding the grossly offensive conditions and treatment of inmates" at McAlester, Bohanon refrained from ordering the penitentiary closed. He concluded that it was in the public interest, and in that of all parties concerned, that the state correctional officers be afforded time to bring the prison into line with constitutional standards. He did, however, retain jurisdiction and made it clear that he would order regular hearings to ensure compliance with the May 30 order. Asked if the ruling could be enforced, Bohanon made it clear that he believed it could and would be. He declared, "It can be enforced. You can't just put a man in a five-by-eight box and tell him he can't exercise . . . say he can't read books . . . deny him medical care." The *Tulsa Daily World* reported, "If the Constitution doesn't work for prison inmates, racial minorities, the impoverished, Bohanon says, it is of no value to anyone." The threat was thus implicit: a massive writ of habeas corpus to release all prisoners being held under unconstitutional conditions if recalcitrant officials refused to obey.[13]

The *Tulsa Tribune* praised the decision. Saying that the state had done an "atrocious job of operating its correction system" and finding conditions at McAlester "substantially worse" than they had been before the riot, the newspaper counseled, "It would be a serious mistake for the state of Oklahoma to use appeals or other tactics to try to avoid the basic changes U.S.

Dist. Judge Luther Bohanon has ordered in operations of the state penitentiary at McAlester." In a supportive editorial, the *Tulsa Daily World* termed the penal system "the Shame of Oklahoma" and said that the only tragedy in the ruling was that it "should be necessary at all."[14] In general, the Tulsa press was more supportive of Bohanon than its Oklahoma City counterpart, which emphasized a negative view. In a 1980 editorial the *Tulsa World* praised Bohanon's actions as "far reaching," saying that they had "prodded Oklahoma to make much-needed correctional improvements which would not have been possible in the normal course of events."[15]

Bohanon believes that then Attorney General Larry Derryberry and Governor David Hall understood the constitutional rationale behind the dictated reforms. Unfortunately, many state legislators (including the man who would succeed Hall as governor, David Boren), the McAlester warden and staff, and the general public received the order "with a high degree of contempt and resistance." Bohanon was seen as exacerbating the problems caused by the riot. As he was in the *Dowell* case, Luther Bohanon was involved once again in a protracted legal battle and at odds with public opinion.

On June 3, 1974, state penal institution officials met for forty-five minutes behind closed doors, discussing Bohanon's order point by point. At the end of the session, the press was admitted, and it was announced that the Department of Corrections would "comply fully" with the ruling. Chairman Ungerman stated, "We're going to comply with each and every provision of Judge Bohanon's ruling. There's not going to be any refusal to cooperate in any matter." The board, how-

ever, had refused to consider the seventh point in the
order, which dealt with the use of chemical agents in
the prisons.[16]

Even a casual review of the press conference reveals
the depth of resentment felt by the penal officials at
the Bohanon order. When asked if the judge had demanded too much of the department in his ruling, Ungerman declined comment, stating merely, "As an
attorney I have no right to criticize a judicial board."
He did go on to state, however, that, had Bohanon refrained from acting, the department would have cor-
rected the complained of conditions within the next
fiscal year. Such a statement cannot help but be regarded as highly disingenous. Many of the abuses and
deficiencies dealt with by Judge Bohanon's order had
continued since the inception of the Oklahoma prison
system. It stretches credulity to believe that, left to its
own devices, the Department of Corrections would
have dealt with them. At the trial, John Grider, acting
director of the corrections department, had testified,
however, that $4.3 million was planned to be spent for
enlarging outlying facilities and other improvements.
Judge Bohanon had called the statement "heartwarm-
ing and encouraging."[17]

In his autobiographical manuscript Bohanon writes,
"After they received copies of my order, the Oklahoma
Department of Corrections and the Oklahoma Attorney General were convinced of the correctness of my
findings, order and judgment. They did not appeal my
order but instead resolved to comply. As a result, in
the following three years great improvements were
made toward bringing the OSP [Oklahoma State Peni-
tentiary] and other places of confinement within constitutional guidelines in the treatment of prisoners."[18]

Improvements in the prison program included increased recreational facilities and the institution of drug abuse groups, ethnic support groups, and a chapter of Alcoholics Anonymous. Restrictions were lifted on mail and reading material. Barber shops were established in each cell block. And new systems were put in place to better protect prisoners and to discourage loan sharking.

ACLU and Civil Rights Division attorneys continued to work with penologists to gather evidence of overcrowding, inadequate medical care, use of force, and other violations of civil rights and civil liberties. Over the next three years, Judge Bohanon held evidentiary hearings every six months to monitor the state's obedience to his decree. By the spring of 1977, conditions in the state incarceration facilities had again reached a critical level. State Senator John Young of Sapulpa undertook an extensive fact-finding tour of the prisons and reported the desperate situation to Governor David Boren. His letter to the state's chief executive went unanswered. When Young got a bill through the legislature authorizing an intensive study of Oklahoma's prison standards, Boren vetoed the law.[19]

Bohanon held a hearing on May 23. Convinced that conditions at the state's incarceration facilities presented "an immediate and intolerable threat to the safety and security of inmates, prison personnel and the people of the State of Oklahoma," Bohanon issued another order in the *Battle* case.[20]

Acknowledging that substantial progress had been made in many areas, the judge nonetheless found that the state had failed to meet constitutional standards in its penal system. He wrote, "Persons are sent to prison as punishment, not *for* punishment." While not finding a constitutional right to rehabilitation, he did find that "it is incumbent on the incarcerating body to provide the individual with a healthy habilitative environment" in which rehabilitation could occur. Instead, in Oklahoma he saw a prison system where overcrowding and unsanitary conditions were pervasive. In one instance, that of the Lexington Regional Training Center, the physical plant had been built during World War II as a facility with an expected useful life of ten years. These buildings were still being used thirty years later. Such circumstances were unlikely to produce rehabilitation of any kind.[21]

Bohanon again demurred from requiring abandonment or closure of any confinement facility and stated that the court did not intend that any inmate should be released prematurely. He did, however, order the defendants to reduce the prison population at McAlester and at the Oklahoma State Reformatory at Granite at rapid rates. He also ordered an end to the packing of inmates into cells and mandated that every prisoner be incarcerated in no less than sixty square feet of cell space or seventy-five square feet of dormitory space.[22]

State officials wasted little time in appealing this order to the Tenth Circuit Court of Appeals. The appellate court's affirmance of Bohanon's order on October 26 had, the judge writes, a "very convincing effect on the matter of constitutional compliance requirements on all prison officials, the State Attorney General, the governor, and especially on the members of State Legislature who now realized their duty to operate the prisons in keeping with constitutional requirements."

Federal judges expect to be obeyed. Thus, almost by definition, when they issue an order directing officials to take some action, they expect it to be the last order that they need to make in that particular matter. It is perhaps this attitude that informs the above assessment. For whatever reason, however, Judge Bohanon was once again prematurely optimistic in his faith that state officials were ready to comply fully with his directives.

On February 7, 1978, Bohanon ordered the ACLU and the Justice Department to report on the level of the state's compliance with his previous dictates in *Battle I* and *II*. The report, made six months later, detailed some progress. Serious and ongoing deficiencies were found, however, in numerous areas addressed by the court's previous decisions. Prisons were still overcrowded. Health care services were still inadequate. Prisoners were still denied meaningful access to the courts.

On September 11, Bohanon issued his *Battle III* decision. In a scathing opinion, he began by quoting at length from his 1977 order. He then retraced the history of the case and of the defendants' compliance with his court's previous decisions. Bohanon clearly had reached the limits of his patience.

The threat that had only been implicit in previous opinions was now made painfully explicit. Within three months, Bohanon charged, the wooden dormitories at the Lexington correctional facility were to be closed. Within ten months, the state legislature would appropriate sufficient funds to replace deficient cell houses at Granite and McAlester or those facilities would be shut down. In any event, the deficient cell blocks were to be permanently closed no later than May 1, 1981. Construction of their replacements had to begin within fourteen months. Obedience to Bohanon's other prior orders was again directed, and tight time schedules were laid down to ensure compliance. The order closed with the familiar quotation from the King James version of the Gospel according to Saint Matthew: "I was in prison, and ye came unto me."[23]

Reaction to this latest decision came swiftly. Amy Hodgins, the assistant attorney general who had argued the state's case, questioned the order's validity. "My defendants [the state correctional officers] are not in the legislature," she pointed out, "and there is no way they can appropriate money." Without help from the legislative body, she stated that her clients were "totally incapable" of complying with the judge's directives.[24]

Governor David Boren, long an opponent of Bohanon, lashed out at the decision and directed Corrections Director Ned Benton and Attorney General Derryberry to begin the appeal process. He stated, "It is my firm intention that the state will appeal. For the state to simply sit back and give in to an order forcing the spending of $50 million of the taxpayers' money is absolutely unthinkable. That will never happen as long as I am the governor of the state of Oklahoma."[25]

Boren's words, which Judge Bohanon underlined in his copy of the *Oklahoma City Times* article on the case, rang hollow when one considered that he was, at the time, a lame duck, locked in a close and heated runoff election for the Democratic nomination for U.S. Senate. Long before the deadline set for legislative appropriation of required funds, David Boren would no longer be governor of the State of Oklahoma.

The night of the decision, in a debate with senatorial opponent Ed Edmondson, Boren called for an end to lifetime appointments for federal judges. Once again, the remarks are highlighted in copies of the newspaper articles about the matter contained in the judge's files. Later, in the Senate, Boren would live up to his campaign promise when he introduced legislation to limit the tenure of judges in the federal judiciary.[26]

Fortunately, cooler heads prevailed. Speaker of the

Oklahoma House of Representatives Bill Willis and Oklahoma Senate President Pro Tempore Gene Howard said that they felt that the legislature had no recourse but to obey the order. Howard announced, "The judge has made his determination as a judicial matter. We must accept it." Although Willis criticized the decision, Howard stated that it would be a "disservice" to all concerned to talk about not following it. Corrections director Benton stated that he felt that the likelihood of success on appeal, which in itself would cost state taxpayers thousands of dollars, was poor. He politely informed the governor that the decision whether or not to appeal rested not with the executive but with him and the other named defendants in Battle's suit.[27]

Over the ensuing years, hundreds of millions of dollars were spent on construction of new institutions and renovation and expansion of existing facilities. As a result of this tremendous effort, the Oklahoma correctional system became the first major system in the country to be fully accredited by the American Correctional Association. Bohanon notes, "Justifiably, governor Nigh could be proud of the accomplishments and announced a goal of expanding this accreditation to every Oklahoma penal institution [McAlester was the first]. The plan received the full support of President Pro Tempore Howard and Speaker Draper, who pledged additional prison funding so long as the extra money did not adversely impact other state agencies." Throughout the period, Bohanon continued to hold regular hearings to audit compliance with his prior orders and issue further directives as necessary when state compliance fell short.[28]

Still, in all, as the appellate court consistently supported Judge Bohanon's positions, steady progress was made. By the spring of 1982, after a personal inspection of McAlester, Bohanon "could find . . . there existed no improper clothing, bedding, coldness, food, hygiene, medication, medical care, or segregation of inmates." Facilities were "modern, clean, well equipped and convenient." Overcrowding had virtually been eliminated. The judge announced that he was "delighted" with conditions, which were better than he could have imagined. Although praising the undertaking of the tour and its outcome, Gaylord papers could not resist an editorial jibe that perhaps it was time for Bohanon to tour Oklahoma City's schools as well.[29]

An unforeseen upsurge in the prison population, however, jeopardized the significant gains made over the years.

The Department of Corrections asked for permission to begin doubling up prisoners in cells. In support of their request they offered a recent Supreme Court case approving such accommodations and the testimony of Ronald C. Marshall, an Ohio correctional officer whose institution had been the subject of the case.[30] Marshall testified that the Oklahoma facilities met or exceeded the standards of the Southern Ohio Correctional Facility of which he was superintendent.

ACLU attorney Louis Bullock disagreed. Characterizing the Oklahoma prisons as "a system in crisis," he claimed that inmates "should not have to wait until the court's conscience was shocked into action by the 'way human beings are being treated in the Oklahoma Prison System.' " In a direct challenge to Bohanon, he said, "We should not be made to sit and subject ourselves to repetition of conditions that we've seen before and wait until that date for this court to intercept the deterioration." Bullock argued that overcrowding of cells was unconstitutional and urged the judge to "put a lock on the door to allow no more increases in population until specific units are brought into line."[31]

Rejecting Bullock's arguments, Judge Bohanon decided to permit the state to double up inmates in cells. In so doing, however, he warned that the overcrowding did place the Oklahoma system in the "twilight" of constitutional compliance, and he again retained jurisdiction over the case. Battle's lawyers quickly appealed to the Tenth Circuit.

The three-judge appellate panel which considered the case agreed that the Oklahoma system was in compliance with the dictates of the Constitution. The three split, however, on the issue of retention of jurisdiction. Judge James Barrett, writing for the circuit court, said that Bohanon had erred in retaining jurisdiction over a system that was in constitutional compliance. Judges Monroe McKay and William Doyle, concurring with the Barrett opinion, disagreed: they maintained that the trial court judge should retain jurisdiction until there was no reasonable expectation that unconstitutional conditions would recur.

With findings and orders in the circuit court's opinion at variance with each other, Judge Bohanon had a "very serious problem." He could relinquish jurisdiction based on the state's good-faith commitments to maintain compliance, but he feared a relapse into unconstitutional conditions. Under the circumstances, he deemed it prudent to recuse himself and submit the case to a disinterested judge. On December 7, 1983, he turned the matter over to Judge Frank Seay, chief judge of the Eastern District of Oklahoma, who after a review of the record concurred that the state had met its constitutional obligations and surrendered jurisdiction.

Thus ended Judge Bohanon's decade-long involvement with the Oklahoma prisons. Over the years

Governor Nigh and the state legislature worked as promised to prevent a recurrence of the conditions which had prevailed before the court's intervention. The Prison Overcrowding Emergency Power Act, which provided safety valves in the event of a state of emergency caused by prison overcrowding, was enacted in 1984 and invoked twenty times between 1984 and 1987 to relieve overcrowding and prevent a return to unconstitutionality.

The *Battle* case, following upon the heels of *Dowell* (and sometimes sharing daily headlines with it), earned Judge Bohanon a reputation as the most liberal and interventionist judge in Oklahoma. Like *Dowell*, it also exposed an intense streak of determination that could cut either for or against civil liberties activists depending upon the circumstances. A colleague accurately described Bohanon to an Associated Press reporter as "a stubborn man who feels strongly about many things and when he is convinced he is right, neither hell nor high water can make him change his mind."[32]

Although he protected the rights of Bobby Battle, Bohanon never met the inmate outside of a courtroom. He noted in an interview that, after release from prison, Battle tried to see him on two occasions, but the judge refused. "I just didn't see any point in that," he said.[33]

Despite his liberal reputation, Bohanon has always considered himself a "Constitutionalist," a strict constructionist who merely follows the Constitution and the mandates of the Supreme Court. Friends agree that he does not regard himself as either liberal or conservative but merely an adherent to the Constitution. Clara Luper, in her autobiography, writes, "It took Judge Luther Bohanon, a strong, strict constitutionist, to destroy all Black and White schools in Oklahoma City."[34]

At the time of his May 30, 1974, order in *Battle*, Bohanon, in words echoing his beloved friend and mentor Dean Monnet, told the press, "I have the deep feeling that our founding fathers created the greatest form of government known to the world. If you remove the Constitution, you remove that form of government." Asked if the founding fathers would be surprised to find out that the document they crafted in Philadelphia guaranteed prisoners thirty-three hundred calories a day and sixty square feet of living space, he laughs and replies, "Yes, I guess they would." But then, he stops laughing and expands upon his response: "They'd be surprised because they didn't live through what we've lived through and haven't seen the horrible abuses that go on. They were men of tremendous morality. If they were alive today, with our modern standards of conduct, I don't think they would disagree."[35]

A similar thought was picked up by columnist Sheryl McCarthy during the battle over confirmation of Clarence Thomas to the Supreme Court when she wrote, "A justice should see the Constitution not just as a set of narrow rules, but as a statement of basic fairness. He or she should envision a society not just as the founding fathers saw it then, but as their principles would require them to see it now." Luther Bohanon agrees.[36]

Chapter VI

The American Indian Land Case

A clash between the obligation of the United States to protect Indian property rights on the one hand and the policy
of forcing their relinquishment on the other was inevitable.
With the passage of the Indian Removal Act of 1830 . . . it
became apparent that policy, not obligation would prevail.
In spite of the promises to protect the Indians' land and sov-
ereignty, it was clear that the United States was unable or
unwilling to prevent the States and their citizens from vio-
lating Indian rights.

CHOCTAW NATION V. OKLAHOMA,
397 U.S. 620 (1970)

It seems to us from a careful reading of Choctaw v. Oklahoma . . . that the Supreme Court by strong implications expressed its views as to title of the Arkansas River bed, and
what it said is not mere suggestion, but amounts to a complete understanding that the tribes, the Choctaws and
Chickasaws on the one hand and the Cherokees on the
other, acquired the river bed in fee by reason of the large
tracts of land granted them for their permanent home, free
of white man's interference.

CHOCTAW NATION V. CHEROKEE NATION,
393 F. Supp. 224 (E.D. Okl. 1975)

FROM time to time the courts are called upon to decide property disputes not between individuals but between sovereign entities. Governments vested with control of specific geographic areas, no less than individual property owners, may argue over exactly where a "fence" ought to be placed. Perhaps the best known of these suits is *United States* v. *Texas,* in which the Supreme Court awarded Greer County to what is now the State of Oklahoma. To reach that decision, Justice Harlan scrutinized diplomatic correspondence, trails and roads, explorations and land grants, and old Spanish and French treaties. Across his opinion's pages pass three presidents of the United States and personages the likes of John C. Calhoun, Sam Houston, and George McClellan. Such a case was *Choctaw Nation* v. *Cherokee Nation,* arising out of a century-long dispute over ownership of the bed of the Arkansas River.[1]

In 1943, as governor of Oklahoma, Robert S. Kerr witnessed the terrible costs of the state's drought-flood-drought cycle, beginning his lifelong commitment to the Arkansas River Navigation Project. For Kerr the project would serve the dual goal of achieving political power through control of public works while at the same time bringing prosperity to his home state. As governor and later as a U.S. senator, he would spearhead the fight to make the last great tributary of the Mississippi navigable.[2]

Kerr's obsession with public works in general—and the Arkansas River project in particular—would lead columnist Drew Pearson to accuse, "Kerr grubs around the pork barrel and would like to transfer anything but the Washington monument to Oklahoma." With wry humor, the Oklahoma senator retorted, "Pearson underestimates my intentions. What more beautiful surroundings could possibly be imagined for that famous monument than our fair state of Oklahoma."[3]

When Kerr began to press for the navigation project, few thought he would succeed. "To the untrained eye the Arkansas River 'looked like a vast sandbed ... a scar on the face of [the] State.' " It was joked that the only way that the Arkansas would be made into a highway of commerce was to pave it. In arguing against the proposal, liberal senator Paul Douglas (D. Ill.) said that "the potential sound of the steamboat whistle was taking away the sanity of men."[4]

President Kennedy liked Kerr because in him the president recognized "many of the hard-driving, power-manipulating instincts" of the president's father, Joseph Kennedy. Thus, according to close Kennedy aide Theodore Sorenson, the president understood exactly what motivated Kerr. Yet even JFK joked that with the staggering sums spent on the project over the years (the estimated federal share exceeding $1.2 billion), it would have been chapter to turn it into "beautiful boulevards."[5]

Still, the idea was not as far-fetched as it might have seemed at first blush. Kerr's biographer, Anne Hodges Morgan, is quick to point out: "During most of the nineteenth century the Arkansas River had been the main highway of the Indian Territory. In the steamboat's heyday, $5 million worth of merchandise had been shipped into Oklahoma river towns. As late as 1870, steam packets from the Mississippi carried men and livestock to the flourishing cattle industry in Kansas."[6]

Those who scoffed at Bob Kerr's Big Ditch underestimated the determination and zeal of the Oklahoma politician. While still governor in 1946, with the help of powerful Oklahoma senator Elmer Thomas, he persuaded Congress to authorize the project, designed to bring shipping up from the Gulf of Mexico to Tulsa and, perhaps later, to Oklahoma City. In 1948, Kerr went to the U.S. Senate and arranged to have himself assigned to the Rivers and Harbors Subcommittee. By 1955 he was that subcommittee's chair, and in 1956 appropriations for the project tripled.[7]

Although the project would not be completed until 1971, eight years after Kerr's death, Kerr saw to it that it was continually authorized during his lifetime and, during the Kennedy administration, used his role as the "new wagon master of the rocky road to the new frontier" to ensure that by the time of his death it was well under way.[8]

After the Arkansas River Navigation Project was begun, a dispute arose about whether Oklahoma or the Indian nations owned the riverbend. According to Judge Bohanon, "The state of Oklahoma had previously claimed the river bottom and had collected $1,000,000 in royalties from the sale of sand and gravel for construction purposes, and oil and gas lease bonuses and royalty payments." In 1966 the Cherokee Nation filed suit against the state and numerous corporations to whom the state had leased oil and gas and other mineral rights along the river. The tribe sought to recover the royalties and to prevent further interference with its property rights, claiming that it had owned the river since 1835. Subsequently, the Choctaws and Chickasaws were granted leave to intervene.[9]

The case eventually reached the Supreme Court in 1970. Justice Thurgood Marshall wrote the opinion for a badly divided Court. After analyzing treaties dating back to "the period immediately after the Revolution-

ary War and prior to the adoption of the Constitution,"
the Court held that the Indians and not the state held
title to the riverbed.[10]

Although the high court had settled the question of
ownership between the state and the Indians, it had
not dealt with the potentially more difficult question
of title among the native nations themselves. Lawyers
for the tribes involved persuaded Speaker of the House
Carl Albert, member of Congress from Oklahoma, to
shepherd a bill through Congress giving the federal
courts jurisdiction to decide the dispute between the
tribes. The Choctaw-Chickasaw-Cherokee Boundary
Dispute Act was passed on December 20, 1973. For
Judge Bohanon the act seemed reminiscent of the special legislation that he had persuaded Mike Monroney
to manage following the Otoe and Missouria claim.[11]

Suit was brought immediately, and on January 28,
1974, Chief Judge David T. Lewis of the Tenth Circuit
Court of Appeals convened a three-judge panel at the
request of Judge Bohanon, to whose docket the case
had originally been assigned. The panel consisted of
Judge William J. Holloway, Jr., Judge Bohanon, and
Judge Fred Daugherty. For Bohanon, who had extensive experience in Indian litigation from his involvement in the Otoe and Missouria case, the matter was a
welcome diversion from preparation for the upcoming
trial in the prison case, *Battle* v. *Anderson*, and from
his ongoing duties with regard to school desegregation.[12]

A one-day trial took place on January 3, 1975. Because the case had originally been assigned to him,
Judge Bohanon was asked to write the opinion. Be-
sides, of the three judges hearing the case, Bohanon
was best suited to undertake the necessarily meticulous review of the record. He notes, "My work on the

Otoe and Missouria case before the Court of Indian Claims gave me a good background in writing the opinion since the case was based primarily on treaties between the government and the Indian Tribes."[13]

Bohanon carefully analyzed the same treaties examined by the Supreme Court in *Choctaw Nation* v. *Oklahoma* and referred back to the cases of *Cherokee Nation* v. *Georgia* and *Worcester* v. *Georgia*, which had first dealt with Cherokee land claims in the 1830s.[14]

In fact, *Worcester* v. *Georgia* had been used in Chief Justice John Marshall as an occasion to review all treaty relations with the Cherokees. He found that the tribe had been denied systematically the rights negotiated by those treaties which guaranteed self-government and the assurance that the laws of the United States would treat Indians "as nations, and manifest a firm purpose to afford that protection which treaties stipulate." As previously noted, both the State of Georgia and President Andrew Jackson defied the decision.[15]

In a carefully crafted opinion in the *Choctaw Nation* v. *Cherokee Nation* case, Judge Bohanon decided title to the riverbed section by section. The court thus divided the land among the involved tribal entities.[16]

Today Judge Bohanon correctly remembers the decision in *Choctaw Nation* v. *Cherokee Nation* as a "significant opinion." Taken together, *Choctaw Nation* v. *Oklahoma* and *Choctaw Nation* v. *Cherokee Nation* trace the sad history of white treatment of the American Indian from a time when "Indian Nations occupied much of what is today the southern and southeastern parts of the United States" to a time when even a small corner of Oklahoma was taken from them. In *Choctaw Nation* v. *Cherokee Nation*,

Judge Bohanon quotes from the Cherokee Treaty of 1828, which begins:

Whereas, it being the anxious desire of the Government of the United States to secure to the Cherokee nation of Indians ... a permanent home, and which shall, under the most solemn guarantee of United States, be, and remain, theirs forever—a home that shall never, in all future time, be embarrassed by having extended around its lines, or placed over it the jurisdiction of a Territory or State, nor be pressed upon by the extension, in any way, of any of the limits of any existing Territory or State.[17]

"All future time" expired less than forty years later when new treaties were forcibly concluded with the Cherokees and the other four of the Five Civilized Tribes as a result of their supposed support for the Confederacy during the Civil War. By those treaties, the Five Civilized Tribes were forced to cede half their lands in Oklahoma. The Algonkians and their Lakota-speaking neighbors (the Osages, the Otoes and Missourias, the Kaws, and the Poncas) agreed to leave their lands in Kansas and moved to the newly open areas in Indian Territory. White settlers then moved into the vacated Kansas land.

Justice Douglas, in his concurring opinion in *Choctaw Nation* v. *Oklahoma*, pointed out the nation's abysmal record in Indian affairs and sounded a clarion call, stating that "only the continuation of a regime of discrimination against these people, which long plagued the relations between the races, can now deny them this just claim."[18] In the two *Choctaw Nation* cases, Congress and the courts worked in tandem to redress one small part of their grievances.

As Judge Bohanon's major cases went, *Choctaw Nation* v. *Cherokee Nation* was relatively calm. It inspired none of the calumny of either the school board case or the prison case. As it concluded, however, another high-profile constitutional case fell to him—the last of a triumvirate of such cases. The defendant against whom citizens were asserting their rights was no longer the Oklahoma City School Board nor even the State of Oklahoma. The alleged violators of the Constitution were now the Department of Health, Education, and Welfare and the U.S. government itself.

Chapter VII

The Laetrile Case

The right of privacy has no more conspicuous place than in the physician-patient relationship, unless it be in the priest-penitent relationship. . . .

The right to seek advice on one's health and the right to place reliance on the physician of one's choice are basic to Fourteenth Amendment values. We deal with fundamental rights and liberties, which, as already noted, can be contained or controlled only by discretely drawn legislation that preserves the "liberty" and regulates only those phases of the problem compelling legislative concern.

DOE *V.* BOLTON,
410 U.S. 179 (1973),
Justice Douglas concurring

This case raises questions of fundamental political and philosophical consequence. Freedom of choice necessarily includes freedom to make a wrong choice, and there is much force to the argument that matters of the type herein under discussion should be left ultimately to the discretion of the persons whose lives are directly involved.

RUTHERFORD *V.* UNITED STATES,
429 F. Supp. 513 (W.D. Okl. 1977)

IN 1830, two French chemists isolated a cyanide-laced drug from bitter almonds. They named their discovery amygdalin, after *amygdala,* the Greek word for almond. The substance was used as early as 1845 for the treatment of cancer. Between 1934 and 1945, it was employed experimentally for that purpose at the University of California Medical School. In 1949, American physician Ernest T. Krebs, Sr., and his son produced a synthetic amygdalin which they called laetrile. The drug is now produced from the pits of apricots and other fruits.[1]

Today the debate continues about laetrile's safeness and effectiveness as a treatment for cancer. The American Medical Association and the Food and Drug Administration (FDA) maintain that the drug is ·wholly ineffective as a cancer treatment and that the cyanide in its structure makes it toxic if not very carefully used. Still, hundreds of cancer patients each year travel outside the United States to receive a drug generally recognized as useless and even potentially harmful. These were the issues presented in *Rutherford* v. *United States,* and it was the rights of those patients that were before the court.

On March 12, 1975, Juanita Stowe and her husband brought suit to prohibit the U.S. government from preventing the importation of laetrile for Mrs. Stowe's use as a treatment for cancer. Oklahoma federal district court judge Fred Daugherty heard and denied Mrs. Stowe's petition. She subsequently died.

Following Mrs. Stowe's death, two other victims, Glen L. Rutherford and Phyllis S. Schneider, along with Mrs. Schneider's husband, filed an amended complaint on behalf of all terminally ill cancer patients and their spouses.[2] Upon the filing of the new complaint, the case was reassigned to Judge Bohanon.

Rutherford had become ill in the summer of 1971 and was diagnosed as suffering from diverticulitis. Subsequent examinations showed, however, that he had an invasive adenocarcinoma, a glandular cancer, and he was scheduled to undergo surgery on December 10, 1971.

"Tremendously upset and concerned about the prospects of surgery and its potential outcome," he failed to report for the operation and traveled instead to Tijuana, Mexico, where he underwent laetrile therapy. Several weeks later, Rutherford was cured. His doctors in Mexico instructed him, however, to continue taking the laetrile.[3]

Between 1972 and 1974, Rutherford apparently successfully obtained laetrile in the United States. In late 1974, however, he received a letter from his supplier stating that his 1975 supply of the drug had been seized by federal authorities and the carrier was in jail, facing a ten-thousand-dollar fine and a possible five-year prison term. Deprived of his chosen method of care and fearing a recurrence of his cancer if the treatments were not continued, Rutherford brought suit against the United States and the secretary of the Department of Health, Education, and Welfare.[4]

On August 14, 1975, Judge Bohanon found that the FDA's procedures made it impossible for ordinary individuals to apply for approval of drugs. Finding that Rutherford was "wholly without means or resources to comply" with the FDA's regulations, he ruled that for cancer patients "to be denied the freedom of choice for treatment by laetrile to alleviate or cure their cancer, was and is a deprivation of life, liberty or property without due process of law guaranteed by the Fifth Amendment to the Constitution of the United States." He then temporarily enjoined the FDA to desist from

precluding the administration of laetrile to those suffering from cancer. Rutherford was allowed to purchase and import a six month supply of the drug.[5]

The FDA immediately appealed to the Tenth Circuit
Court of Appeals, arguing that it had no duty to ap-
prove a drug unless an application were filed, that it
was not empowered to determine by itself the safety or
efficacy of the drug, and that Bohanon had overstepped
his power in entering an injunction which blocked enforcement of an act of Congress without convening a
three-judge panel. The appellate court ruled, however,
that Bohanon was within his authority. Split two-to-
one, the circuit court did not reach the constitutional
or statutory issues presented by the trial court's opinion. Instead, finding the FDA's record "grossly inadequate," it affirmed the injunction and remanded the
matter to Bohanon for a determination whether or not
laetrile was a "new drug" within the meaning of the
Food, Drug, and Cosmetics Act and thus subject to regulation pursuant to that act.[6]

Bohanon held the hearing ordered by the court of appeals on December 30, 1976, rendering a further opinion in January 1977. Finding, as had the appellate court
before him, that an adequate administrative record did
not exist with regard to the FDA's decision concerning
laetrile, he requested that the agency make available to
him the written basis for its determination, "no matter
how casual or unstructured its form or content might
be." When he was advised that no such rationale existed in any form, an outraged Bohanon declared,
"Clearly, federal agencies may not rule by fiat invok-
ing only some unexplained application of their own
expertise in defense of policy decisions they have
made." Declaring the agency's actions to be "arbi-
trary" and "capricious," he referred the matter back to

them for further study, ordering that they report back within 120 days. In the meantime, the injunction was continued.[7]

In his January 4 opinion, Bohanon determined that the action should be certified as a class action (that is, that the plaintiffs could sue not only on their own behalf but also on the behalf of all those similarly situated). The matter came back before him on March 18, when the plaintiffs petitioned the judge to clarify who exactly was to be included in the class; they urged that it include "all victims of cancer and their spouses who are responsible for the cost of treatment." The government argued for its part that class certification was improper. It argued that early diagnosis and prompt treatment are critical to the cure of cancer and that needless deaths would occur if cancer patients forewent conventional treatment in favor of laetrile.[8]

The judge issued his order on April 8. He rejected the defendants' argument concerning timely treatment, writing: "Such arguments have little applicability to the fraction of cancer patients whose lives orthodox medical science professes no capacity to preserve. To speak of laetrile as being 'unsafe' for these people is bizarre." He continued: "It is connotative of a paternalism incompatible with this nation's philosophy as to the proper relationship between the government and its citizenry." He did agree, however, to limit the plaintiff class to all "terminally ill cancer patients."[9] The defendants did not appeal the class certification.

Two and a half months later, on July 29, 1977, after two days of hearings and compilation of over fifty-five hundred pages of written testimony, the commissioner of the FDA announced the agency's official findings. He stated that laetrile was not generally recognized as a safe and effective medicine to combat cancer and that it was, in fact, a "new drug" not exempt from the approval requirements of the FDA by virtue of the grandfather provisions of the Food, Drug, and Cosmetics Act. He concluded that distribution of the drug laetrile was therefore illegal and subject to the regulation of the FDA. The plaintiffs immediately challenged the agency's decision, arguing that laetrile was not a new drug and that the FDA prohibition on its use violated the plaintiffs' right under the U.S. Constitution.[10]

With all the issues now squarely joined, Bohanon held a hearing and issued his decision. His lengthy, heavily footnoted opinion, issued on December 5, 1977, is a model of the judicial craft. Beginning with a meticulous history of laetrile as a medicine, he concluded that it was not a new drug and was eligible to be "grandfathered" under the appropriate provisions of the Food, Drug, and Cosmetics Act. He then turned to the constitutional right of privacy to which he had made only passing allusion in earlier opinions.

Acknowledging that the FDA was doing the job with which it had been charged by Congress, Bohanon stated that he did not doubt either the agency's good intentions or its desire to protect the public. "It is never easy," he wrote, "for one who is concerned and feels himself knowledgeable to observe others exercise their freedom in ways that to him appear unenlightened." He went on: "Nonetheless, our political ideals emphasize that the right to freely decide is of much greater significance than the quality of those decisions actually made." He reiterated his belief that the United States as a nation, "historically and continuously," had been "irrevocably committed to the principle that the individual must be given maximum latitude in determining his [or her] own personal destiny." He concluded that denial of use of a nontoxic

substance in connection with a person's own health of-
fended the constitutional right of privacy.[11]

Even if no such privacy right existed generally, Bohanon argued, the use of laetrile by terminally ill persons
who had exhausted orthodox approaches or who used
laetrile in conjunction with more conventionally recognized methods of treatment would be protected. He
declared:

To be insensitive to the very fundamental nature of the civil
liberties at issue in this case, and the fact that making the
choice, regardless of its correctness, is the sole prerogative of
the person whose body is being ravaged, is to display slight
understanding of the essence of our free society and its constitutional underpinnings. This is notably true where, as
here, there are no simple answers or obvious solutions, uncertainty is pervasive, and even the best efforts leave so
much to be desired.[12]

The government was permanently enjoined from interfering with the importation or use of laetrile for the
treatment of cancer. The U.S. Customs Service was
also ordered to distribute information to its employees
within twenty days to ensure compliance. The next
day, the *Oklahoma Journal* opened with a large head-
line in red reading, "Bohanon: Laetrile Legal."

An appeal was taken again to the Tenth Circuit,
which heard arguments on January 26, 1978. Six
months later, a unanimous panel handed down its decision. The court once again declined to reach the constitutional arguments advanced by Bohanon. It agreed,
however, that "safe" and "effective" were meaningless
terms when applied to a drug employed by the terminally ill. It approved the permanent injunction issued
by the lower court but limited it only to intravenous

injections administered by licensed physicians on persons certified to be terminally ill.

The government appealed once more, and, following denial of a petition for a rehearing by the Tenth Circuit, on August 8 petitioned the U.S. Supreme Court for a writ of certiorari. The petition was granted, and on April 25, 1979, Solicitor General Wade McCree argued the government's case to the high court.

On June 18, Justice Thurgood Marshall spoke for a unanimous court, which concluded that safety and efficacy were not necessarily meaningless even when applied to those terminally ill. A drug was as unsafe, they concluded, for the terminally ill as for anyone else if its potential for inflicting death or physical injury was not offset by the possibility of therapeutic benefit. Marshall noted that although the circuit court's opinion was limited to laetrile, the reasoning could not be so easily confined. If safety and effectiveness had no place as standards regarding treatment for the terminally ill, then the FDA was powerless to regulate any drug, however toxic or ineffective. Fearing a return to the days when "resourceful entrepreneurs ... advertised a wide variety of purportedly simple and painless cures for cancer, including liniments of turpentine, mustard oil, eggs and ammonia; peat moss; arrangements of colored floodlamps; pastes made of glycerin and limburger cheese; mineral tablets; and 'Fountain of Youth' mixtures of spices, oil, and suet," the high court overturned the Tenth Circuit's decision and remanded the case to the appellate court. Because the intermediate court did not reach the privacy issue, the nine justices likewise declined to address it.[13]

The Supreme Court here explicitly disagreed with Judge Bohanon's analysis. He had faced the fraud issue squarely in his opinion, writing: "This court's decision

in this case in no way portends the return of the traveling snake oil salesman. As emphasized earlier, the
right to use a harmless, unproven remedy is quite distinct from any alleged right to promote such. FDA is
fully empowered under other statutory provisions to
combat false or fraudulent advertising of ineffectual or
unproven drugs."[14]

Faced with a declaration by the Supreme Court that
there could be no exceptions to the drug act for the terminally ill, on February 10, 1980, the Tenth Circuit re-
luctantly dealt with the constitutional and statutory
issues. It found that the higher court's opinion im-
pliedly rejected the privacy claim with regard to use of
laetrile and held accordingly. In its brief opinion, the
circuit court also raised questions about the act's
grandfather clauses and dissolved Bohanon's injunctions, remanding to him for further findings. The
plaintiffs applied to the Supreme Court for a second
writ of certiorari, but the Court rejected the plea.[15]

Bohanon held additional hearings and again determined that laetrile was exempt from "new drug" clas-
sification by virtue of the grandfather clauses. On
remand he therefore, as he had once before in the
school board case, reinstated his original injunction.
On this occasion, however, the ploy failed. On April 6,
1983, the Court of Appeals ordered the district court to
dissolve the injunction and dismiss the complaint.

Bohanon complied and dismissed Rutherford's case
on March 2, 1984, but ten days later allowed Rutherford's attorneys to file an amended complaint. The
government rushed their case up to the higher court in
Denver, asking that the Court of Appeals issue a writ
of mandamus against Bohanon for refusing to follow
its earlier order. The appellate court declined to issue
the writ, arguing that the district court judge *had* com-

plied with its order. The court found further, however, that Bohanon had erred in allowing the case reopened. On December 9, 1986, it ordered again that he dismiss the complaint and discontinue all injunctions.[16] The judge unhappily complied.

Rutherford v. *United States* thus came to an end, twelve years after it was originally filed. Although he would continue to supervise the school board case and his decision ending discrimination in the Oklahoma National Guard, *Rutherford* would prove to be Judge Bohanon's last new major case.

During its pendency, Bohanon steadfastly refused to discuss the *Rutherford* case, even declining a profile on CBS's *60 Minutes*. His reluctance continues today, motivated in no small measure by the fact that he was reversed. In his autobiography, he makes no mention of *Rutherford*. But when asked about his controversial decision for a 1978 magazine profile, he remarked, "Any time you clothe a man with power and he's afraid to use it for fear of reprisal, you don't have a judge. A judge should determine what the law is, what the facts are and act accordingly. He should not determine what the public says or thinks."[17]

Judge Bohanon ultimately was reversed in *Rutherford*. His efforts to permanently enjoin the FDA from banning importation of an unproven drug failed. His opinions in the case, however—particularly the first (399 F. Supp. 1208) and last (438 F. Supp. 1287)—clearly set forth his views on the constitutional right of privacy. When asked from what source the right of privacy springs—whether it is to be found in the First Amendment, the Ninth Amendment, or the penumbra to the Bill of Rights—Bohanon, like Justice William O. Douglas, located it in the person's fundamental "right to be let alone."[18]

These opinions rank as perhaps the most creative and carefully argued of the progeny of *Roe* v. *Wade*, and they once again are being studied by scholars and civil liberties lawyers as *Roe* and the right it articulated come under increasing attack. They are especially important because, with their implicit libertarian analysis, they have much in consonance with neoconservative theories of governmental deregulation.[19]

A strong advocate of the principal of *stare decisis*, Bohanon contends that once a precedent becomes settled and the right has been relied upon, it should not be overturned. In this regard, he believes that although *Roe* may be cut back, it should not be overturned. It is, however, emblematic of the controversy over the right of privacy generally, and *Roe* specifically, that Clarence Thomas, nominated to the Supreme Court by President George Bush, praised a 1987 article which called the right, as articulated by *Roe*, a "spurious right born exclusively of judicial supremacy with not a trace of lawful authority." Thomas termed the article "a splendid example of applying natural law."[20] Such persons would do well to read Judge Bohanon's opinions in *Rutherford* v. *United States* and note their libertarian approach.

In the end, the plaintiffs in *Rutherford* lost. But they had won twelve years, and twelve years in the life of a cancer patient can be an eternity. Today, Bohanon notes with obvious pride that Glen Rutherford is still alive and living in Kansas. The two still keep in occasional contact.[21]

When asked if, stricken with cancer, he would use laetrile to fight the disease, Bohanon replied, "I certainly would."[22]

Epilogue

A biographer constantly worries that he or she is merely producing "a musty bit of sidelight on a [generally] long-dead, relatively obscure local hero." The "naughty little secret" of historians, however, is a good story. The life of Luther Bohanon is such a story. Like the heroes of his youth—Webster, Lincoln, Monnet—his influence will be felt well beyond his lifespan. "Only now in the twilight of his career," says Bohanon's former law partner Bert Barefoot, Jr., "are many of his peers recognizing his impact on the State of Oklahoma."[1]

The portrait of Judge Bohanon that emerges from a study of his legal career is that of a complex man. Like many judges, he has an almost pathological aversion to being reversed, yet when convinced of the rightness of his position, he has taken actions that all but dared higher courts to reverse his decisions. He is a fiercely stubborn man who at times perhaps let pride cloud his judgment. He is a liberal Democrat who has taken some of the most activist positions in the history of the judiciary, yet he considers himself apolitical. By his own admission, he is perhaps best described as an inadvertent civil libertarian.[2] In spite of these very human foibles, however, or perhaps because of them, he ranks as one of the ablest jurists this country has produced. As Bert Barefoot, Jr., agreed, "Without doubt history will recognize him as a courageous and honest judge devoted to the American way of life as it should be now and hereafter."[3]

It is said that Judge Learned Hand once called in one of his law clerks and asked, "Sonny, to whom am I responsible? No one can fire me. No one can dock my pay. Even those nine bozos in Washington, who sometimes reverse me, can't make me decide as they wish. Everyone should be responsible to someone. To whom am I responsible?" The young man shrugged and waited. Then Hand turned and pointed at the volumes of reported cases that made up his law library. He said, "To those books about us. That's to whom I am responsible."[4]

Judge Bohanon echoed this sentiment of Hand, another proponent of the religious theory of the law, in the aftermath of the prison case *Battle* v. *Anderson*: "Politicians must listen to the people or they lose their jobs. A judge has a different responsibility . . . it is to the Constitution." He stated, "A federal judge's first concern is what the Constitution is and is it being violated. Most people have a firm conviction that the wishes of a majority should be the law of the land. The wishes of the majority must bend when the Constitution comes into play. The Constitution wasn't written just to protect the majority; it was written for protection of minorities . . . and they are the Negroes, the Indians, the illiterate, the poor."[5]

In the end, for those who would expand the boundaries of civil rights and civil liberties in the United States, perhaps what is needed is a Supreme Court populated by people like Earl Warren who constantly ask, "Is that what the United States *should* stand for?" and lower courts peopled by persons like Bohanon and Hand who sensitively treat, follow, and, if necessary, massage precedent. Learned Hand said that a judge "must preserve his authority by cloaking himself in the majesty of an overshadowing past, but he must discover some composition with the dominant needs of his times." Years later, Archibald Cox, his former clerk, wrote, "The law, even as it honors the past, must reach for justice of a kind not measured by force, by the pressures of interest groups, nor even by votes, but only by what reason and a sense of justice say is right."[6]

For seventy years, first as a lawyer and later as a judge, Luther Bohanon has been responsible to "those books" while at the same time seeking to discover the dominant needs of his times. He has sought simply to do what was right. That is perhaps the greatest compliment that can be paid to someone who dedicated his life, however imperfect, to the law and, through it, to the service of his fellow human beings.

Appendix

PUBLISHED OPINIONS
OF LUTHER L. BOHANON

Where possible, the citation from Federal Supplement or Federal Reporter, 2d Series, has been given. Where opinions appear in more than one reporting service, no parallel citations are provided.

1962

Goldberg v. *Gable,* 45 Lab. Cas. (CCH) par. 3.303 (D. Kan. 1962).

McAdams Drilling Company v. *United States,* 62-2 U.S. Tax Cas. (CCH) par. 9812 (N.D. Okl. 1962).

Fuqua v. *Gulf, Colorado and Santa Fe Railway Company,* 206 F. Supp. 812 (E.D. Okl. 1962).

Arthur v. *K. D. Emerick Well Servicing Company,* 209 F. Supp. 491 (E.D. Okl. 1962).

Division No. 892, Amalgamated Association of Street, Electric Railway & Motor Coach Employees of America v. *M.K. & O. Transit Lines, Inc.,* 210 F. Supp. 351 (N.D. Okl. 1962).

Oil, Chemical & Atomic Workers International Union, Lo-

cal 5-283 v. *Arkansas Louisiana Gas Company,* 211 F. Supp. 780 (W.D. Okl. 1962).

1963

Atlas Life Insurance Company v. *United States,* 216 F. Supp. 457 (N.D. Okl. 1963).

Citizens Bank of Booneville v. *National Bank of Commerce,* 217 F. Supp. 193 (N.D. Okl. 1963).

Carribean Mills, Inc. v. *McMahon,* 217 F. Supp. 639 (N.D. Okl. 1963).

Zebco Company v. *United States,* 218 F. Supp. 441 (N.D. Okl. 1963).

Dowell v. *School Board of the Oklahoma City Public Schools,* 219 F. Supp. 427 (W.D. Okl. 1963).

Sinclair Oil & Gas Company v. *Brown,* 220 F. Supp. 106 (E.D. Okl. 1963).

Harding v. *Cameron,* 220 F. Supp. 466 (W.D. Okl. 1963).

Tidewater Oil Company v. *Penix,* 223 F. Supp. 215 (E.D. Okl. 1963).

Day v. *Hartford Accident & Indemnity Company,* 223 F. Supp. 953 (N.D. Okl. 1963).

Hillyer v. *Pan American Petroleum Corporation,* 225 F. Supp. 425 (N.D. Okl. 1963).

1964

Botsford v. *City of Norman,* 226 F. Supp. 258 (W.D. Okl. 1964).

Jordan Petroleum Company v. *United States,* 64-1 U.S. Tax Cas. (CCH) par. 9486 (W.D. Okl. 1964).

Hendershot v. *Cobra Services, Inc.,* 64-1 U.S. Tax Cas. (CCH) par. 4404 (W.D. Okl. 1964).

Simler v. *Canner,* 228 F. Supp. 127 (W.D. Okl. 1964).

Tipton v. *Bready,* 229 F. Supp. 301 (E.D. Okl. 1964).

Goodwin v. *Thomas,* 232 F. Supp. 193 (W.D. Okl. 1964).

First National Bank & Trust Company of Oklahoma City v.

United States Fidelity and Guaranty Company, 232 F. Supp. 927 (W.D. Okl. 1964).
Isbell v. *Osgood,* 234 F. Supp. 602 (E.D. Okl. 1964).
Pearce v. *United States,* 236 F. Supp. 431 (W.D. Okl. 1964).

1965

Busby v. *U.S. Steel Corporation,* 237 F. Supp. 602 (E.D. Okl. 1965).
Ward v. *Page,* 238 F. Supp. 431 (E.D. Okl. 1965).
Thomas v. *Brown,* 239 F. Supp. 350 (E.D. Okl. 1965).
Barber v. *Page,* 239 F. Supp. 265 (E.D. Okl. 1965).
Anderson v. *Town of Forest Park,* 239 F. Supp. 576 (W.D. Okl. 1965).
Kessinger v. *Oklahoma,* 239 F. Supp. 639 (E.D. Okl. 1965).
United States v. *United States Fidelity & Guaranty Company,* 240 F. Supp. 316 (N.D. Okl. 1965).
United States v. *Massey,* 65-2 U.S. Tax Cas. (CCH) par. 9570 (W.D. Okl. 1965).
United States v. *85.11 Acres of Land, More or Less, Situated in Pawnee County,* 243 F. Supp. 423 (N.D. Okl. 1965).
Bennett v. *United States,* 266 F. Supp. 627 (W.D. Okl. 1965).
Dowell v. *School Board of Oklahoma City Public Schools,* 244 F. Supp. 971 (W.D. Okl. 1965).
United States v. *Pyle,* 248 F. Supp. 40 (E.D. Okl. 1965).
Wirtz v. *White,* 53 Lab. Cas. (CCH) par. 31,756 (N.D. Okl. 1965).

1966

Culp v. *Northwestern Pacific Indemnity Company,* 248 F. Supp. 675 (N.D. Okl. 1966).
Stout v. *United States,* 66-1 U.S. Tax Cas. (CCH) par. 9279 (W.D. Okl. 1966).
Cannon v. *Willingham,* 358 F.2d 719 (10th Cir. 1966).
Carpenter v. *Crouse,* 358 F.2d 701 (10th Cir. 1966).
Smoake v. *Willingham,* 359 F.2d 386 (10th Cir. 1966).
Webb v. *Crouse,* 359 F.2d 394 (10th Cir. 1966).
Blair v. *Crouse,* 360 F.2d 28 (10th Cir. 1966).

Wirtz v. *Triple "AAA" Company, Inc.,* 53 Lab. Cas. (CCH) par. 31,787 (W.D. Okl. 1966).

Keeton v. *United States,* 256 F. Supp. 576 (D. Colo. 1966).

Rosenfield v. *Kay Jewelry Stores, Inc.,* 256 F. Supp. 898 (W.D. Okl. 1966).

General Adjustment Bureau, Inc. v. *General Insurance Adjustment Company,* 258 F. Supp. 535 (N.D. Okl. 1966).

Wirtz v. *Universal Advertising Service,* 258 F. Supp. 542 (N.D. Okl. 1966).

1967

R. V. McGuinness Theatres v. *Video Independent Theatres,* 262 F. Supp. 607 (N.D. Okl. 1967).

Republic Supply Company v. *Sunset Drilling Company,* 264 F. Supp. 50 (W.D. Okl. 1967).

Finch v. *United States,* 263 F. Supp. 309 (W.D. Okl. 1967).

Wirtz v. *Bledsoe,* 54 Lab. Cas. (CCH) par. 31,888 (N.D. Okl. 1967).

Appleton v. *Kennedy,* 268 F. Supp. 22 (N.D. Okl. 1967).

Goldman v. *United States,* 273 F. Supp. 137 (W.D. Okl. 1967).

1968

Wirtz v. *Mistletoe Express Service, Inc.,* 57 Lab. Cas. (CCH) par. 32,003 (W.D. Okl. 1968).

Asenap v. *United States,* 283 F. Supp. 566 (W.D. Okl. 1968).

Independent School District 93, Pottawatomie County v. *Western Surety Company,* 280 F. Supp. 367 (W.D. Okl. 1968).

United States v. *Weissman,* 280 F. Supp. 367 (W.D. Okl. 1968).

Wirtz v. *Triple "AAA" Company, Inc.,* 57 Lab. Cas. (CCH) par. 32,035 (W.D. Okl. 1968).

Walker v. *United States,* 68-1 U.S. Tax Cas. (CCH) par. 9370 (W.D. Okl. 1968).

Wirtz v. *Stanley Home Products, Inc.,* 58 Lab. Cas. (CCH) par. 32,057 (N.D. Okl. 1968).

Rinehart v. *United States*, 68-2 U.S. Tax Cas. (CCH) par. 9553 (W.D. Okl. 1968).

Board of Education of Independent School District 20, Muskogee County v. *Oklahoma*, 286 F. Supp. 845 (W.D. Okl. 1968).

Oklahoma Gas & Electric Company v. *United States*, 289 F. Supp. 98 (W.D. Okl. 1968).

Bailey v. *United States*, 291 F. Supp. 800 (W.D. Okl. 1968).

Wirtz v. *Greenshaw Supermarket, Inc.*, 59 Lab. Cas. (CCH) par. 32,128 (W.D. Okl. 1968).

1969

Craig v. *Champlin Petroleum Company*, 300 F. Supp. 119 (W.D. Okl. 1969).

Dailey v. *City of Lawton*, 296 F. Supp. 266 (W.D. Okl. 1969).

Goodwin v. *Page*, 296 F. Supp. 1205 (E.D. Okl. 1969).

Green v. *Ford Motor Company*, 70 L.R.R.M. 3180 (W.D. Okl. 1969).

Shultz v. *Mistletoe Express Service, Inc.*, 60 Lab. Cas. (CCH) par. 32,168 (W.D. Okl. 1969).

Phillips Pipe Line Company v. *United States*, 299 F. Supp. 768 (W.D. Okl. 1969).

Shultz v. *Lincoln Rock Corporation*, 60 Lab. Cas. (CCH) par. 32,190 (E.D. Okl. 1969).

Erwin v. *United States*, 302 F. Supp. 693 (W.D. Okl. 1969).

Shultz v. *Kelley*, 61 Lab. Cas. (CCH) par. 32,245 (E.D. Okl. 1969).

Oklahoma, ex rel. Wilson v. *Blankenship*, 308 F. Supp. 870 (W.D. Okl. 1969).

1970

Harrington v. *United States*, 70-1 U.S. Tax Cas. (CCH) par. 9215 (N.D. Okl. 1970).

Dowell v. *Board of Education of Oklahoma City Public Schools*, 307 F. Supp. 583 (W.D. Okl. 1970).

Kasmeier v. *Chicago, Rock Island and Pacific Railroad Company*, 74 L.R.R.M. 2767 (W.D. Okl. 1970).

Christmas v. *El Reno Board of Education, Independent School District No. 34*, 313 F. Supp. 618 (W.D. Okl. 1970).

1971

Oklahoma Publishing Company v. *National Sportsmen's Club, Inc.*, 323 F. Supp. 929 (W.D. Okl. 1971).
Markham v. *State Farm Mutual Automobile Insurance Company*, 326 F. Supp. 39 (W.D. Okl. 1971).
In the Matter of Four Seasons Nursing Centers of America, Inc., 329 F. Supp. (W.D. Okl. 1971).
Buck v. *United States*, 72 U.S. Tax Cas. (CCH) par. 9372 (N.D. Okl. 1971).

1972

Dowell v. *Board of Education of Oklahoma City Public Schools*, 338 F. Supp. 1256 (W.D. Okl. 1972).
In the Matter of Public Leasing Corporation, 344 F. Supp. 754 (W.D. Okl. 1972).
Burden v. *United States*, 72-2 U.S. Tax Cas. (CCH) par. 9597 (N.D. Okl. 1972).
Gordon v. *Laborers' International Union of North America*, 351 F. Supp. 824 (W.D. Okl. 1972).
Hodgson v. *Stockmans Livestock Commission Company, Inc.*, 70 Lab. Cas. (CCH) par. 32,824 (W.D. Okl. 1972).
Federal Deposit Insurance Corporation v. *Boone*, 361 F. Supp. 133 (W.D. Okl. 1972).

1973

In the Matter of Four Seasons Nursing Centers of America, Inc., 357 F. Supp. 594 (W.D. Okl. 1973).
Umdenstock v. *American Mortgage & Investment Co. of Oklahoma City*, 363 F. Supp. 1375 (W.D. Okl. 1973).
In the Matter of Traders Compress Company, 1974 Trade Cas. (CCH) par. 75,425 (W.D. Okl. 1973).
Paddington Corporation v. *Major Brands, Inc.*, 359 F. Supp. 1244 (W.D. Okl. 1973).

Ashland Oil, Inc. v. *Phillips Petroleum Company*, 364 F. Supp. 6 (N.D. Okl. 1973).

United States v. *Ed Lusk Construction Company, Inc.*, 74-1 U.S. Tax Cas. (CCH) par. 9225 (E.D. Okl. 1973).

1974

Halliburton Company v. *Dow Chemical Company*, 182 U.S.P.Q. (BNA) 178 (N.D. Okl. 1974).

Reserve National Insurance Company v. *United States*, 74-1 U.S. Tax Cas. (CCH) par. 9486 (W.D. Okl. 1974).

Battle v. *Anderson*, 376 F. Supp. 402 (E.D. Okl. 1974).

Oklahoma Publishing Company v. *Powell*, 22 Fair Empl. Prac. Cas. (BNA) 1418 (W.D. Okl. 1974).

Daiflon, Inc. v. *Allied Chemical Corporation*, 64 F.R.D. 690 (W.D. Okl. 1974).

Scenic Rivers Association of Oklahoma v. *Lynn*, 382 F. Supp. 69 (E.D. Okl. 1974).

Brennan v. *Myers*, 78 Lab. Cas. (CCH) par. 33,374 (W.D. Okl. 1974).

1975

J. E. and L. E. Mabee Foundation, Inc. v. *United States*, 389 F. Supp. 673 (N.D. Okl. 1975).

Morales v. *Reading & Bates Offshore Drilling Co.*, 392 F. Supp. 41 (N.D. Okl. 1975).

Choctaw Nation v. *Cherokee Nation*, 393 F. Supp. 224 (E.D. Okl. 1975).

Fanning v. *School Board of Independent School District #23 of Jefferson County*, 395 F. Supp. 18 (W.D. Okl. 1975).

Rutherford v. *United States*, 399 F. Supp. 1208 (W.D. Okl. 1975).

Maryland Casualty Company v. *Turner*, 403 F. Supp. 907 (W.D. Okl. 1975).

Sentry Insurance v. *Longacre*, 403 F. Supp. 1264 (W.D. Okl. 1975).

Covey v. *C.I.T. Corporation*, 71 F.R.D. 487 (E.D. Okl. 1975).

1976

Fabian v. *Independent School District No. 89 of Oklahoma County,* 409 F. Supp. 94 (W.D. Okl. 1976).

Dowell v. *Board of Education of Independent School District No. 89 of Oklahoma County,* 71 F.R.D. 49 (W.D. Okl. 1976).

Sprague v. *United States,* 76-2 U.S. Tax Cas. (CCH) par. 9566 (W.D. Okl. 1976).

Health Systems Agency of Oklahoma, Inc. v. *Norman,* Lexis, slip opinion, June 11, 1976 (W.D. Okl. 1976).

National Labor Relations Board v. *Heyman,* 541 F.2d 796 (9th Cir. 1976).

Franke v. *Midwestern Oklahoma Development Authority,* 428 F. Supp. 719 (W.D. Okl. 1976).

Lowery v. *Hauk,* 422 F. Supp. 490 (C.D. Cal. 1976).

1977

Rutherford v. *United States,* 424 F. Supp. 105 (W.D. Okl. 1977).

Health Systems Agency of Oklahoma, Inc. v. *Norman,* No. CIV-76-0215-B, Slip Opinion, January 21, 1977 (W.D. Okl. 1977) (available on Lexis).

Rutherford v. *United States,* 429 F. Supp. 506 (W.D. Okl. 1977).

Sparks v. *Wyeth Laboratories, Inc.,* 431 F. Supp. 411 (W.D. Okl. 1977).

Oklahoma Publishing Company v. *Walsh,* 22 Fair Empl. Prac. Cas. (BNA) 1427 (W.D. Okl. 1977).

Battle v. *Anderson,* 447 F. Supp. 516 (E.D. Okl. 1977).

United States v. *Sor-Lokken,* 557 F.2d 775 (10th Cir. 1977).

Wessely Energy Corporation v. *Arkansas Louisiana Gas Company,* 438 F. Supp. 360 (W.D. Okl. 1977).

United States v. *Brinklow,* 560 F.2d 1003 (10th Cir. 1977).

United States v. *Brinklow,* 560 F.2d 1008 (10th Cir. 1977).

Securities and Exchange Commission v. *Haswell,* 1977 Fed. Sec. L. Rep. (CCH) par. 97,156 (W.D. Okl. 1977).

Star Oil Company, Inc. v. *United States,* 78-1 U.S. Tax Cas. (CCH) par. 9160 (W.D. Okl. 1977).

Rutherford v. *United States,* 438 F. Supp. 1287 (W.D. Okl. 1977).

1978

Thornton v. *Coffey,* 17 Fair Empl. Prac. Cas. (BNA) 725 (W.D. Okl. 1978).

Neeley v. *American Fidelity Assurance Company,* 17 Fair Empl. Prac. Cas. (BNA) 482 (W.D. Okl. 1978).

Sprague v. *United States,* 78-2 U.S. Tax Cas. (CCH) par. 9650 (W.D. Okl. 1978).

Battle v. *Anderson,* 457 F. Supp. 719 (E.D. Okl. 1978).

Ashland Oil, Inc. v. *Phillips Petroleum Company,* 463 F. Supp. 619 (N.D. Okl. 1978).

1979

Circle v. *Jim Walter Homes, Inc.,* 470 F. Supp. 39 (W.D. Okl. 1979).

First American Bank and Trust Company v. *United States,* 79-1 U.S. Tax Cas. (CCH) par. 9205 (W.D. Okl. 1979).

Peacock v. *Board of Regents of the Universities and State College of Arizona,* 597 F.2d 163 (9th Cir. 1979).

Professional Systems & Supplies Co., Inc. v. *Databank Supplies & Equipment Co., Inc.,* 202 U.S.P.Q. (BNA) 693 (W.D. Okl. 1979).

Coffman v. *Ljungkull,* 205 U.S.P.Q. (BNA) 56 (W.D. Okl. 1979).

Marshall v. *Coastal Growers Association,* 598 F.2d 521 (9th Cir. 1979).

1980

United States v. *Zink,* 612 F.2d 511 (10th Cir. 1980).

United States v. *Thomas,* 613 F.2d 787 (10th Cir. 1980).

Smith v. *Equitable Life Assurance Society,* 614 F.2d 720 (10th Cir. 1980).

United States v. *Burns,* 624 F.2d 95 (10th Cir. 1980).

Plastic Container Corporation v. *Continental Plastics of Oklahoma, Inc.,* 515 F. Supp. 834 (W.D. Okl. 1980).

1981

Lindley v. *Amoco Production Company,* 639 F.2d 671 (10th Cir. 1981).

Missouri-Kansas-Texas Railroad Company v. *Early,* 641 F.2d 856 (10th Cir. 1981).

Plastic Container Corporation v. *Continental Plastics of Oklahoma, Inc.,* 515 F. Supp. 834 (W.D. Okl. 1981).

Hays v. *Murphy,* 521 F. Supp. 1290 (E.D. Okl. 1981).

1982

Battle v. *Anderson,* 541 F. Supp. 1061 (E.D. Okl. 1982).

Lyon v. *United States,* 94 F.R.D. 69 (W.D. Okl. 1982).

1983

Navaho Tribe v. *Bank of New Mexico,* 700 F.2d 1285 (10th Cir. 1983).

1984

Dolan v. *Project Construction Corporation,* 725 F.2d 1263 (10th Cir. 1984).

Perrell v. *Financeamerica Corporation,* 726 F.2d 654 (10th Cir. 1984).

Vakas v. *Rodriguez,* 728 F.2d 1293 (10th Cir. 1984).

Seattle–First National Bank v. *Carlsteadt,* 1984 Fed. Sec. L. Rep. (CCH) par. 91,499 (W.D. Okl. 1984).

Hill v. *Heckler,* 592 F. Supp. 1198 (W.D. Okl. 1984).

Hill v. *Heckler,* No. CIV-84-734-B, Slip Opinion, August 30, 1984 (W.D. Okl. 1984) (available on Lexis).

United States v. *McConnell,* 749 F.2d 1441 (10th Cir. 1984).

Helms v. *Independent School District No. 3 of Broken Arrow,* 750 F.2d 820 (10th Cir. 1984).

1985

United States v. *Broce,* 753 F.2d 811 (10th Cir. 1985).

Greer v. *Heckler,* 756 F.2d 794 (10th Cir. 1985).

United States v. *Swingler,* 758 F.2d 477 (10th Cir. 1985).

Dowell v. *Board of Education of the Oklahoma City Public Schools,* 606 F. Supp. 1548 (W.D. Okl. 1985).

Charczuk v. *Commissioner of Internal Revenue,* 771 F.2d 471 (10th Cir. 1985).

Easton v. *City of Boulder,* 776 F.2d 1441 (10th Cir. 1985).

Federal Deposit Insurance Corporation v. *TWT Exploration Company, Inc.,* 626 F. Supp. 149 (W.D. Okl. 1985).

1986

O'Rourke v. *City of Norman,* 640 F. Supp. 1451 (W.D. Okl. 1986).

O'Rourke v. *City of Norman,* No. CIV-85-10-B, Slip Opinion, decided May 7, 1986, filed July 18, 1986 (W.D. Okl. 1986) (available on Lexis).

Tenneco Oil Company v. *Bogert,* 630 F. Supp. 961 (W.D. Okl. 1986).

Salazar v. *Heckler,* 787 F.2d 527 (10th Cir. 1986).

1987

Cox v. *Murray Ohio Manufacturing Company,* 1987 U.S. Dist. Lexix 14907 (W.D. Okl. 1987).

Seattle–First National Bank v. *Carlsteadt,* 678 F. Supp. 1543 (W.D. Okl. 1987).

Rosebud Coal Sales Company v. *Weigand,* 831 F.2d 926 (10th Cir. 1987).

Dowell v. *Board of Education of the Oklahoma City Public Schools,* 677 F. Supp. 1503 (W.D. Okl. 1987).

1988

Allstate Insurance Company v. *Thomas,* 684 F. Supp. 1056 (W.D. Okl. 1988).

Combined Communications Corporation of Oklahoma, Inc. v. *Boger,* 689 F. Supp. 1065 (W.D. Okl. 1988).
United States v. *Young,* 862 F.2d 815 (10th Cir. 1988).

1989

Kelley v. *Rivl Manufacturing Company,* 704 F. Supp. 1039 (W.D. Okl. 1989).
Firstier Mortgage Co. v. *Investors Mortgage Insurance Co.,* 708 F. Supp. 1224 (W.D. Okl. 1989).

1990

Cox v. *Murray Ohio Manufacturing Company,* 732 F. Supp. 1555 (W.D. Okl. 1990).
Jordan v. *United States,* 740 F. Supp. 810 (W.D. Okl. 1990).

1991

Scheerer v. *Rose State College,* 774 F. Supp. 620 (W.D. Okl. 1991).
Sanchez v. *Philip Morris Inc.,* 774 F. Supp. 626 (W.D. Okl. 1991).
Ferguson v. *Prudential Ins. Co. of America,* 777 F. Supp. (W.D. Okl. 1991).
Dowell v. *Board of Education,* 778 F. Supp. 1144 (W.D. Okl. 1991).

1992

Prince v. *Farmers Insurance Company, Inc.,* 790 F. Supp. 263 (W.D. Okl. 1992).
Tatum v. *Philip Morris Incorporated,* No. CIV-90-1485-B, Slip Opinion (W.D. Okl. 1992).

Notes

FOREWORD

1. *Battle* v. *Anderson*, 457 F. Supp. 719 (1978).

PREFACE

1. Malcolm Muggeridge, *A Third Testament* (New York: Ballantine Books, 1976), 1.

2. A full listing of Judge Bohanon's published opinions is contained in the appendix. I hope that someday a compendium of Bohanon's opinions will be published in an easily accessible form such as the treatment given by Vern Countryman to the opinions of Justice Douglas in his *The Douglas Opinions* (New York: Random House, 1977).

3. Dean Kovaleff is the author of numerous books and articles on modern diplomatic, legal, and economic history. He is best known for his book and articles on relations between business and government during the Eisenhower administration.

4. Professor Bankwitz is widely recognized as the doyen of modern French historians. His best-known book is *Maxime Weygand and Civil-Military Relations in Modern France* (Cambridge, Mass.: Harvard University Press, 1967). He is currently at work on a biography of French prime minister Pierre-Etienne Flandin and on "Betrayal of Honor: French Civil-Military Relations in the 20th Century."

Professor Alexander has taught at Oxford and held fellowships at Yale and the Sorbonne. He is the author of *The French and Spanish Popular Fronts: Comparative Perspectives* (with Helen Graham) (Cambridge: Cambridge University Press, 1989) and *The Republic in Danger: Maurice Gamelin, the Defence of France and the Politics of French Rearmament* (Cambridge: Cambridge University Press, 1992). He is a member of the faculty of the University of Southampton in Britain.

Professor Washington is the author of *A Testament of Hope: The Essential Writings of Martin Luther King, Jr.* and a leading authority on African-American history. He is currently at work on a book-length religious history of the civil rights movement.

I. INVISIBLE TAPESTRY

1. *Brown* v. *Board of Education of Topeka, Kansas*, 98 F. Supp. 797 (D. Kan. 1951).

2. *Briggs* v. *Elliot*, 98 F. Supp. 529 (E.D. S.C. 1951). See also the dissent of Justice Rutledge in *Sipuel* v. *Board of Regents*, discussed herein.

3. Luther Bohanon interview with author, Nov. 13, 1988. See chapter 7 herein for a fuller discussion of the right of privacy as articulated by *Roe*.

4. Learned Hand, "Mr. Justice Cardozo," 52 Harv. L. Rev. 361 (1939).

5. When the Supreme Court declared in *Worcester* v. *Georgia* that Cherokee lands in Georgia belonged to the tribe and were free from white encroachment, President Andrew Jackson said, "The Chief Justice has made the law; now let him try to enforce it." District courts should have provided that enforcement. The Cherokees were removed from Georgia to Oklahoma at bayonet point. One-fourth of the Cherokee Nation died en route.

6. Archibald Cox, *The Court and the Constitution*, 372.

7. Derrick Bell, *And We Are Not Saved: The Elusive Quest for Racial Justice*, 11.

8. Cox, *Court and Constitution*, 183.

9. Learned Hand, "Mr. Justice Cardozo," 52 Harv. L. Rev. 361 (1939).

10. Federal judges are appointed for life. When district judges retire, they become senior judges. Although retired, they are allowed

to retain the cases they have at retirement and to hear such additional cases as they and the court may determine.

David Davis, a capable jurist, served on the Supreme Court from 1862 until 1877. Today he is all but forgotten. A close friend of Lincoln's, and executor of his estate, Davis nonetheless broke with the executive branch and authored the Court's opinion in *Ex parte Milligan*, which proscribed the executive's right to suspend the writ of habeas corpus in wartime. He resigned from the Court in 1877 to become a member of the U.S. Senate, of which he later served as president pro tempore.

Tom McMichael and Keith Coplin, "Luther Bohanon," *Logos*, 1974, p. 8. Bohanon also has pictures of John Kennedy, Robert S. Kerr, and Mike Monroney (the president who appointed him, the senator who recommended him, and a senator who stood by him in many battles) on the wall opposite his desk.

11. *Anderson* v. *Town of Forest Park*, 239 F. Supp. 576 (W.D. Okl. 1965); *Dailey* v. *City of Lawton*, 296 F. Supp. 266 (W.D. Okl. 1969); *Thornton* v. *Coffey*, 17 Fair Empl. Prac. Cas. (BNA) 725 (W.D. Okl. 1978).

On October 25, 1972, schoolteacher Judith Fabian filed *Fabian* v. *Independent School District No. 89*, 409 F. Supp. 94 (W.D. Okl. 1976), alleging that the school district's mandatory maternity leave policy violated Title VII of the Civil Rights Act of 1964. Under the policy, pregnant teachers were either terminated or suspended three months before the anticipated birth of their children. They were not allowed to apply for reinstatement until three months after delivering their babies. This enforced leave of absence was without pay, and teachers were not allowed to accumulate sick leave. In a terse opinion, Bohanon wrote simply, "The mandatory maternity leave policy established by the defendants . . . constitutes prohibited discrimination based on sex."

12. Bohanon interview with author, May 23, 1980.

13. McMichael and Coplin, "Luther Bohanon," 9.

14. *Dowell* v. *Board of Education of Oklahoma City*, 430 F.2d 865 at 868, 869 (10th Cir. 1970).

15. *Who's Who in America*, 1980, 343–44.

16. Matt. 25:35–36.

17. Cox, *Court and Constitution*, 67, 342. The introduction of the constitutional amendment was the fulfillment of a campaign promise made by Boren in his first run for the U.S. senate. The

promise had been made in response to one of Judge Bohanon's most severe orders in the prison reform case, *Battle* v. *Anderson*.

Concerning the election of federal judges, see, for example, Martin Hauan, *He Buys Organs for Churches, Pianos for Bawdy Houses*, 171.

18. Murray Kempton, "Judging Thomas on His Balance," *New York Newsday*, July 3, 1991, p. 13.

19. Sam Ervin, Jr., "Separation of Powers, Judicial Independence," 35 Law and Contemp. Probl. 108, 121 (1970). Ervin, country lawyer and U.S. senator, experienced the importance of separation of powers firsthand as chair of the special Watergate committee.

20. I *Annals of Congress* 439 (1789).

21. James Kent, *Commentaries on American Law*, 1:274, 275–76. Chancellor Kent, known as the American Blackstone, produced his commentaries between 1826 and 1830. They have had a permanent influence upon the American law.

22. Paul L. Ford, ed., *The Writings on Thomas Jefferson*, 4:257, quoted in Cox, *Court and Constitution*, 372.

23. Cox, *Court and Constitution*, 372.

24. Ibid., 374.

II. A LIFE AT LAW

1. Archibald Cox, *The Court and the Constitution*, 377; William Young lecture, Oct. 19, 1982.

2. Bohanon interview with author, Nov. 16, 1988.

3. The six children born to William and Telia before Luther were Edith (b. 1888), Agnes Allie (b. 1889), Elmer Joseph (b. 1891), Mary Rebecca (b. 1893), Charles Herbert (b. 1897), and Ernest Cecil (b. 1899). Three children would be born to William and his second wife after Luther.

4. Luther Lee Bohanon, "The Autobiography of Judge Luther L. Bohanon," manuscript (1988), I-3. Because the manuscript autobiography is largely unavailable to readers, I will cite only significant direct quotes from it. Throughout this book, quotations from Judge Bohanon not otherwise identified come from this autobiography.

5. Ibid.

6. Ibid., I-5–I-6.

7. Bohanon correspondence with author, Feb. 6, 1989.

8. Bohanon, "Autobiography," XII-1.

9. Bohanon interview with author, Nov. 15, 1988.

10. Jim Henderson, "Bohanon Accepts Ill Will of Tough Rulings," *Tulsa World*, June 16, 1974, p. 1.

11. Bohanon, "Autobiography," II-11.

12. Bohanon interview with author, Nov. 15, 1988.

13. Ibid., Nov. 13, 1988.

14. Bohanon correspondence with author, Apr. 4, 1989.

15. Ibid., Nov. 18, 1988.

16. Kenny A. Franks and Paul F. Lambert, *The Legacy of Dean Julien C. Monnet: Judge Luther Bohanon and the Desegregation of Oklahoma City's Public Schools*, 4, 5.

17. Cox, *Court and Constitution*, 26, 181.

18. Sheldon Novick, *Honorable Justice: The Life of Oliver Wendell Holmes*, 205; Cox, *Court and Constitution*, 181; David Danelski and Joseph Tulchin, eds., *The Autobiographical Notes of Charles Evans Hughes*, 144; Liva Baker, *The Justice from Beacon Hill: The Life and Times of Oliver Wendell Holmes*, 216–17, 431. In fact, Holmes himself launched the movement that was to become legal realism in 1881 with publication of his monumental work, *The Common Law*.

19. Franks and Lambert, *Legacy*, 5.

20. Ibid., 126–27. For a more complete discussion of the so-called Grandfather Clause, see chapter 4 herein.

21. Ibid., 124, 127.

22. Novick, *Honorable Justice*, 10, n. 19.

23. "Commemorative Devotion: University of Oklahoma College of Law, Class of 1927, in Honor of Educators Who Give Man His Tomorrow," inscription on base of statue of Dean Julien C. Monnet, University of Oklahoma Law Center, Norman, Oklahoma.

24. Franks and Lambert, *Legacy*, 17. Bohanon's graduating class was the last to be admitted to the Oklahoma bar without having to take the bar examination.

25. Bohanon, "Autobiography," IV-3; James R. Green, *Grass-Roots Socialism: Radical Movements in the Southwest, 1895–1943*, 402.

26. Bohanon interview with author, Nov. 14, 1988; Transcript of the swearing in and robing of Honorable Luther L. Bohanon as Judge of the United States District Court for the Western, Northern, and Eastern Districts of the State of Oklahoma, United States Courthouse, Oklahoma City, Okla., Sept. 11, 1961, p. 13.

27. William C. Kellough, "Power and Politics of the Oklahoma Federal Court," *Chronicles of Oklahoma*, Summer 1987, 194; see also "History United States District Court Western District of Oklahoma," unpublished manuscript prepared by and for the court in Oklahoma; Bohanon correspondence with author, Apr. 18, 1989.

28. Kellough, "Power and Politics," 194.

29. Ibid; John Joseph Mathews, *Life and Death of an Oilman: The Career of E. W. Marland*, 254–55; Bohanon interview with author, Nov. 14, 1988. Gore, in fact, was never much of a factor in the Senate race of 1936. He lost much of his support because of his increasing conflict with President Roosevelt, whom he considered a "pantywaist."

30. Transcript of the swearing in and robing, p. 13.

31. Kellough, "Power and Politics," 194. According to Martin Hauan, Phillips probably would not have become governor without Kerr's support. Phillips, however, did not support Kerr for governor four years later. The pair parted company over Franklin Roosevelt's New Deal; Kerr was for it, and Phillips was not. Hauan, *He Buys Organs for Churches, Pianos for Bawdy Houses*, 160. According to Kerr biographer Anne Hodges Morgan, Phillips's disaffection also contributed significantly to Josh Lee's defeat by Republican E. H. Moore in the senatorial election. Anne Hodges Morgan, *Robert S. Kerr: The Senate Years*, 17.

32. Bohanon interview with author, May 21, 1989.

33. For a complete discussion of *Otoe and Missouria Tribe of Indians* v. *United States*, see Berlin Basil Chapman, *The Otoes and Missourias*. Dr. Chapman provided expert testimony at the trial of the matter.

34. T. H. Watkins, *Righteous Pilgrim: The Life and Times of Harold L. Ickes 1874–1952*, 9–21, 203–205, 530–48; Naomi Bliven, "Say Not the Struggle Naught Availeth," *New Yorker*, Jan. 28, 1991, 91. Collier also would author a history of the Native Americans, *Indians of the Americas*.

35. Bohanon, "Autobiography," VI-3.

36. Ibid., VI-3–VI-4; Watkins, *Righteous Pilgrim*, 542.

37. Martin Hauan, *How to Win Elections Without Hardly Cheatin' At All*, 283–88; Charles C. Alexander, *The Ku Klux Klan in the Southwest*, 229, 247.

38. Bohanon interview with author, Nov. 14, 1988.

39. Watkins, *Righteous Pilgrim*, 547; Chapman, *Otoes and Missourias*, 234–35.

40. Chapman, *Otoes and Missourias*, 234–35.

41. Ibid., 237.

42. Ibid., 272.

43. Bohanon interview with author, Nov. 13, 1988.

44. William A. Berry, manuscript prepared as a foreword for an earlier incarnation of this volume. Quoted remarks are from that piece.

45. Bohanon, "Autobiography," VII-14.

46. See Robert J. Young, *In Command of France*, and Jean-Baptiste Duroselle, *La Décadence: 1932–1939*.

47. Berry, manuscript.

48. Note found in private papers of Judge Bohanon.

III. THE JUDGE

1. Arthur M. Schlesinger, Jr., *Robert Kennedy and His Times*, 373.

2. Martin Hauan, *He Buys Organs for Churches, Pianos for Bawdy Houses*, 155–56; Anne Hodges Morgan, *Robert S. Kerr: The Senate Years*, 205.

3. Robert Dallek, *Lone Star Rising: Lyndon Johnson and His Times, 1908–1960*, 579.

4. Morgan, *Kerr*, 205–206; Hauan, *He Buys Organs*, 156.

5. Morgan, *Kerr*, 206.

6. Bohanon interview with author, Nov. 13, 1988.

7. Susan Heinze Ray interview with author, Oct. 1, 1990. In an interview on July 26, 1990, Bohanon stated that, although "K.G." was dead at the time the judge penned his memoirs, he still wanted to protect his name. The reversal of the initials was a further attempt to disguise his identity.

8. Schlesinger, *Robert Kennedy*, 373.

9. Morgan, *Kerr*, 218; Schlesinger, *Robert Kennedy*, 373.

10. Morgan, *Kerr*, 219.

11. Hauan, *He Buys Organs*, 156; Eugene McCarthy, *Up 'Til Now*, 70; Bohanon correspondence with author, Jan. 23, 1990.

12. Schlesinger, *Robert Kennedy*, 375; taped interviews with Anthony Lewis, Dec. 1964, in the archives of the John F. Kennedy Library, Boston, Mass.; Hauan, *He Buys Organs*, 147.

13. Schlesinger, *Robert Kennedy*, 374; Hauan, *He Buys Organs*, 149, 171; McCarthy, *Up 'Til Now*, 70–71; Booth Mooney, *LBJ: An Irreverent Chronicle*, 53–54.

14. Morgan, *Kerr*, 219; Hauan, *He Buys Organs*, 171. When he was preparing his autobiography, Judge Bohanon confused Arthur Schlesinger's name with that of Seigenthaler and inquired of Schlesinger whether he had not been sent by Attorney General Kennedy to inquire into Bohanon's qualifications (Bohanon to Schlesinger, Sept. 22, 1988). Schlesinger responded that it had not been he but that he believed that it was Seigenthaler whom Kennedy had dispatched (Schlesinger to Bohanon, Oct. 17, 1988).

15. Hauan, *He Buys Organs*, 171; unpublished notes in Bohanon private papers; Bohanon interview with author, Nov. 13, 1988.

16. Jim Henderson, "Bohanon Accepts Ill Will of Tough Rulings," *Tulsa World*, June 16, 1974, p. 4; Hauan, *He Buys Organs*, 156, 176–84.

17. Morgan, *Kerr*, 219.

18. Ibid.

19. Ibid., 219–20.

20. Ibid.

21. Hauan, *He Buys Organs*, 171.

22. Schlesinger, *Robert Kennedy*, 375; Bohanon, "Autobiography," XII-6.

23. Transcript of the swearing in and robing of Honorable Luther L. Bohanon as Judge of the United States District Court for the Western, Northern, and Eastern Districts of the State of Oklahoma, United States Courthouse, Oklahoma City, Okla., Sept. 11, 1961, p. 13.

24. Schlesinger, *Robert Kennedy*, 374.

25. Taped interviews with Anthony Lewis. Kennedy was speaking of both Bohanon and Judge William H. Cox, a friend and recommendation of Senator James O. Eastland of Mississippi. He was also speaking generally of certain other difficult judicial appointments while he was attorney general. See also Edwin O. Guthman and Jeffrey Shulman, eds., *Robert Kennedy in His Own Words*, 107–19.

26. Schlesinger, *Robert Kennedy*, 375; letter from Schlesinger to Bohanon, Oct. 17, 1988.

27. Frosty Troy, "Oklahoman of the Year: Judge Luther Bohanon," *Oklahoma Observer*, Jan. 25, 1984, p. 1.

28. Ibid.

29. Hauan, *He Buys Organs*, 171.

30. Ibid., 5–6, 8; David Craighead, "J. D. to Enter Prison Today," *Oklahoma Journal*, Nov. 21, 1969, p. 2.

31. Katherine Hatch, "McCarty Loses His Appeal for Review by High Court," *Daily Oklahoman*, Oct. 14, 1969, pp. 1, 2; Frosty Troy, "The Trial That Was Exemplary," *Tulsa Tribune*, July 29, 1967, p. 1; Craighead, "J. D. to Enter Prison," 2.

32. Troy, "The Trial," 1. Judge Bohanon's conduct, always characterized as "no nonsense," has not always been universally praised. In 1974, he was twice reprimanded by the Oklahoma Bar Association for criticizing juries that returned verdicts with which he disagreed. Henderson, "Bohanon Accepts Ill Will," 1.

33. Troy, "The Trial," 1; Katherine Hatch, "McCarty Lawyers Claim Law Unfair," *Daily Oklahoman*, July 6, 1969, pp. 1–2. In charging the jury, Judge Bohanon advised, "As a general rule, it is reasonable to infer that a person ordinarily intends all of the natural and probable consequences of acts knowingly done or knowingly omitted. So unless the evidence in this case leads the jury to a different or contrary conclusion, the jury may draw the inference and find that the accused intended all of the natural and probable consequence. . . ." This type of supposedly burden-shifting jury instruction is often a source of controversy in criminal cases.

34. Hatch, "McCarty Loses," 1–2.

35. Bohanon interview with author, Jan. 19, 1991; Craighead, "J. D. to Enter Prison," 1; Hauan, *He Buys Organs*, 5.

36. Bohanon interviews with author, Nov. 13–16, 1988; Kenny A. Franks and Paul F. Lambert, *The Legacy of Dean Julien C. Monnet: Judge Luther Bohanon and the Desegregation of Oklahoma City's Public Schools*, 7; Meacham quote in Troy, "Oklahoman," 15.

37. Oklahoma House of Representatives, Citation, July 3, 1979; Oklahoma Senate, Citation, June 11, 1979.

38. Jerald C. Walker (President, OCU) to Bohanon, July 18, 1990; Marian P. Opala to Bohanon, July 1990; Bohanon to author, Nov. 30, 1990; Mindy Harris-Silk to Bohanon, Oct. 8, 1990; Hardy Summers to Bohanon, Nov. 29, 1990.

39. Bohanon interviews with author, Nov. 13, 1988, and Jan. 19, 1991; Troy, "Oklahoman," 15.

IV: THE SCHOOL BOARD CASE

1. Derrick Bell, *And We Are Not Saved: The Elusive Quest for Racial Justice*, 107. In an interview with the author, Greenberg remembers the statement differently: he recalls that he said that

there was a period of trench warfare during which "progress was slow and dirty and measured by inches." Jack Greenberg interview with author, Feb. 6, 1991. Julius Chambers, current director of the NAACP Legal Defense Fund, agrees with his predecessor, Greenberg. He states, "There was a period of trench warfare of which the school board cases were a part." Julius Chambers interview with author, Mar. 15, 1991.

2. *Dowell* v. *Board of Education,* 71 F.R.D. 49, 56 (W.D. Okl. 1976).

3. Danney Goble, *Progressive Oklahoma: The Making of a New Kind of State,* 115, 124.

4. Ibid., 132–33, 134.

5. Ibid., 135, 137; George Lynn Cross, *Blacks in White Colleges: Oklahoma's Landmark Cases,* 26; Howard Davis, "Luther Bohanon: The Man Behind the Bench, Controversial Judge Turning the Tide," *Oklahoma City Times,* Aug. 20, 1970, p. S1.

6. Cross, *Blacks,* 28–29; Constitution of the State of Oklahoma, Article XIII, Sec. 3. The definition of "white children" was, of course, of particular importance because of Oklahoma's large American Indian population.

In his inaugural address to the constitutional convention, presiding officer William H. Murray urged:

We should adopt a provision prohibiting marriages of negros with other races in this State, and provide for separate schools and give the Legislature power to separate them in waiting rooms and on passenger coaches, and all other institutions in the State. We have no desire to do the negro an injustice. We shall protect him in his real rights. . . . We must provide the means for the advancement of the negro race, and accept him as God gave him to us and use him for the good of society. As a rule they are failures as lawyers, doctors and in other professions. He must be taught in the line of his own sphere, as porters, bootblacks and barbers and many lines of agriculture, horticulture and mechanics in which he is an adept, but it is an entirely false notion that the negro can rise to the equal of a white man in the professions or become an equal citizen to grapple with public questions. . . . I doubt the propriety of teaching him in the public schools to run for office or to train him for professions, but his training should be equal so far as appropriations of funds are concerned to that of any other race, but he should be taught agriculture, mechanics and industries that would make him a being serviceable to society. At the same time let us provide in the Constitution that he shall have equal rights before the courts of the country, that he shall have whatever is due him but teach him that he must lean upon himself, rise by his own exertions, hew out his own destiny as an integral but separate element of the society of the State of Oklahoma.

William H. Murray, "Address to Oklahoma Constitutional Convention," Nov. 20, 1906.

7. Joseph B. Thoburn and Muriel H. Wright, *Oklahoma: A History*, 2:644–45; C. Vann Woodward, *The Strange Career of Jim Crow*, 3d rev. ed., 101–102, 118; Allan Saxe, "Protest and Reform: The Desegregation of Oklahoma City" (Ph.D. diss., University of Oklahoma, 1969), 15; Frosty Troy, "Searching for Culprits: The Busing Inferno," *Oklahoma Observer*, Sept. 25, 1972, p. 1. Troy wrote, "The social fabric of the capital city is seared by flames and everybody wonders who started the fire."

8. Cross, *Blacks*, 6–8; *Wallace* v. *City of Norman*, 9 Okla. 339, 60 P. 108 (1900); Catherine A. Barnes, *Journey from Jim Crow: The Desegregation of Southern Transit*, 13–17; *McCabe* v. *Atchison, Topeka & Santa Fe Railway Co.*, 235 U.S. 151 (1914).

9. *Guinn* v. *United States*, 238 U.S. 347 (1915); Thoburn and Wright, *Oklahoma*, 2:655–56.

10. Saxe, "Protest and Reform," 58; Louise Carol Stephens, "The Urban League of Oklahoma City, Oklahoma" (Ph.D. diss., University of Oklahoma, 1957), 32. Dunjee was also a founder of the Oklahoma Constitutional League, which sought to redress constitutional violations.

11. Saxe, "Protest and Reform," 58.

12. Kaye M. Teall, *Black History of Oklahoma—A Resource Book*, 198; George Lynn Cross, *Professors, Presidents & Politicians: Civil Rights and the University of Oklahoma, 1890–1968*, 124.

13. Stephens, "Urban League," 41–42, 211; Cross, *Blacks*, 24.

14. Saxe, "Protest and Reform," 72–74, 83, 84–85; Stephens, "Urban League," 87; Bell, *And We Are Not Saved*, 111.

15. Cross, *Blacks*, 30–31.

16. Ibid., 31.

17. Ibid., 35–38. Cross provides the best complete histories of *Sipuel* v. *Board of Regents*, 332 U.S. 631 (1948), and *McLaurin* v. *Board of Regents*, 339 U.S. 637 (1950), that currently exist. As a

memoir of one of the principals involved, Cross's book is of special value.

18. Ibid., 43–45.

19. Ibid., 92. Both *Sipuel* and *McLaurin*, in fact, are cited in the *Brown I* decision. For an excellent general discussion of the cases, see Richard Kluger, *Simple Justice*.

20. Bohanon interviews with author, Nov. 13–16, 1988; *Dowell* v. *Board of Education*, 219 F. Supp. 427, 434 (W.D. Okl. 1963). Bohanon interview with author, Nov. 13, 1988. Chief Justice Warren would disagree about *Brown*, saying to Bohanon that he considered the establishment of the principle of one person–one vote to have been of greater importance. See *Baker* v. *Carr*, 369 U.S. 186 (1962) and *Reynolds* v. *Sims*, 377 U.S. 533 (1964).

21. Kluger, *Simple Justice*, 737, 742. Ralph Abernathy, close associate of Martin Luther King, was quick to point out in his autobiography that *Brown* did not end segregation in southern schools, but in Kansas, "the state that contributed the most Union dead in the Civil War. Those of us who had spent our lives in Mississippi and Alabama did not necessarily believe that the same thing could be accomplished in our part of the country. Though we were told the law would apply equally throughout the land, we were skeptical. We had heard that before." Ralph David Abernathy, *And the Walls Came Tumbling Down*, 114.

22. Martin Hauan, *He Buys Organs for Churches, Pianos for Bawdy Houses*, 43–48; Jim Bradshaw, "City Schools Reflect on 25 Years under Brown Decision: Officials Say Integration Has Left Relatively Few Scars," *Oklahoma City Times*, May 11, 1979, p. 1; Clara Luper, *Behold the Walls*, 244; Morgan, England, Humphreys, *Oklahoma Politics*, 56.

23. Bradshaw, "City Schools," 1; Saxe, "Protest and Reform," 131–34; Luther Lee Bohanon, "The Autobiography of Judge Luther L. Bohanon," unpublished manuscript (1988), X-3; Stephens, "Urban League," 150.

24. *United States* v. *Board of Education of Independent School District No. 1, Tulsa County*, 429 F.2d 1253 (10th Cir. 1970). Judge Fred Daugherty, one of the members of the three-judge panel in *Dowell*, dismissed a suit by the U.S. attorney general to require desegregation of the Tulsa public schools on the grounds that the city was constitutionally employing a "neighborhood school attendance plan." The appellate court reversed the decision as "inconsistent with current constitutional standards." For a discussion of

both the Oklahoma City and Tulsa cases (as well as other educational desegregation cases), see Leon Jones, *From Brown to Boston: Desegregation in Education 1954–1974*, vol. 2, *Legal Cases and Indexes*.

25. J. W. Peltason, *Fifty-eight Lonely Men: Southern Federal Judges and School Desegregation*, 9–10. Judge Bohanon concurs that Peltason captured the problems he encountered in the Oklahoma City school case. Bohanon correspondence with author, Apr. 18, 1989.

26. Bell, *And We Are Not Saved*, 111.

27. *Dowell*, 219 F. Supp. at 434; Kenny A. Franks and Paul F. Lambert, *The Legacy of Dean Julien C. Monnet: Judge Luther Bohanon and the Desegregation of Oklahoma City's Public Schools*, 22; Scot W. Boulton, "Desegregation of the Oklahoma City School System," *Chronicles of Oklahoma*, Summer 1980, p. 195.

28. See Saxe, "Protest and Reform."

29. Carl R. Graves, "The Right to Be Served: Oklahoma City's Lunch Counter Sit-ins," *Chronicles of Oklahoma*, Summer 1981, p. 152; for an eloquent description of what it was like to grow up in a segregated Oklahoma City, see Ralph Ellison, *Going to the Territory*, 113–44. A long-time figure in the Oklahoma City movement, Clara Luper is best known for her role in the sit-ins. She also led demonstrations during the 1969 sanitation workers' strike, was a plaintiff in *Dowell*, ran for the U.S. Senate, and edited the magazine *Black Voices*.

30. Graves, "Right to Be Served," 153. Luper also remembered stories of Roscoe Dunjee eating in a segregated diner by posing as an Indian chief. Luper, *Behold*, viii–ix.

31. Graves, "Right to Be Served," 153; Luper, *Behold*, 8–14; Aldon Morris, *The Origins of the Civil Rights Movement: Black Communities Organizing For Change*, 125, 190.

Sit-ins had occurred at lunch counters as early as the 1940s. Manning Marable, *Race, Reform and Rebellion: The Second Reconstruction in Black America, 1945–1982*, 26. This may be considered the first sit-in of what is normally termed the civil rights movement, taking place a year and a half before those in Greensboro (widely thought of as the first). Lerone Bennett, Jr., *Before the Mayflower: A History of Black America*, 5th rev. ed., 556; Howell Raines, *My Soul Is Rested*, 38. Within a short space of time, sit-ins occurred in Tulsa; Stillwater; Enid; East Saint Louis, Illinois; and Wichita, Kansas.

Sociology professor Aldon Morris, *Origins*, 193, states that Luper was the person upon whom these sit-ins pivoted. He writes, "In short, the first sit-in cluster occurred in Oklahoma in 1958 and spread to cities within a 100-mile radius through established organizational and personal networks. The majority of these sit-ins were (1) connected rather than isolated, (2) initiated through organizations and personal ties, (3) rationally planned and led by established leaders, and (4) supported by indigenous resources. Thus the Greensboro sit-ins of February 1960 did not mark the movement's beginning but were a critical link in the chain."

32. Luper, *Behold*, 10; Graves, "Right to Be Served," 154, 155; Harry Golden, *Only in America*, 121–22.

33. Graves, "Right to Be Served," 160–61; Bohanon interviews with author, Nov. 13–16, 1988.

34. Howard Davis, "Integration Just Happened: 'Quality' is Pleasant Hill's Key," *Oklahoma City Times*, Aug. 28, 1969, pp. 1–2.

35. *Dowell*, 219 F. Supp. at 436.

36. "Busing Has Been A Necessary Evil," *Sunday Oklahoman*, May 24, 1981, p. 27; Luper, *Behold*, 244, 232.

37. For a discussion of the NAACP's use of three-judge panels, see Kluger, *Simple Justice*.

38. *Dowell*, 219 F. Supp. at 447.

39. Bohanon, "Autobiography," X-5–X-6; Bohanon interviews with author, Nov. 13–16, 1988.

40. Boulton, "Desegregation," 201. For more information about segregation in housing in Oklahoma, see *Anderson* v. *Forest Park*, 239 F. Supp. 576 (W.D. Okl. 1965), and *Dailey* v. *City of Lawton*, 296 F. Supp. 266 (W.D. Okl. 1969).

41. Boulton, "Desegregation," 203; *Dowell* v. *Board of Education*, 244 F. Supp. 971, 978 (W.D. Okl. 1965).

42. Hauan, *He Buys Organs*, 174.

43. Rex Harlow, *Oklahoma Leaders: Biographical Sketches of the Foremost Living Men of Oklahoma*, 37.

44. Luther Bohanon, "A Word from the Wise Did Not Work," unpublished article, 1988.

45. "The Role of the Press," *Saturday Oklahoman & Times*, Jan. 22, 1977, p. 10.

46. Franks and Lambert, *Legacy*, 41.

47. Ibid., 47.

48. Ibid., 49.

49. Howard Davis and Kathy Christie, "Justice Mulls School Plea; Word Promised: Race Plan Foes Gain Attention," *Oklahoma City Times,* Aug. 29, 1969, pp. 1–2; Franks and Lambert, *Legacy,* 65; Mike Brake, "Schools Confused on Which Plan," *Daily Oklahoman,* Aug. 30, 1969, p. 1; "City Students' Fate Pondered: '. . . We Don't Know What to Do,' Lillard Says," *Oklahoma City Times,* Aug. 30, 1969, p. 1; "New Ruling Puts Schools in Spin, Bohanon's Plan Back in Saddle: 'Tragic Dilemma,' Lillard Says," *Oklahoma Journal,* Aug. 30, 1969, p. 1; Jones, *From Brown to Boston,* 1860–61.

50. Murrah to Bohanon, Aug. 30, 1969; Franks and Lambert, *Legacy,* 66; Bohanon interview with author, Jan. 20, 1992. Not wishing to see another repeat of the events of August 1969, NAACP LDF attorneys, in fact, raised questions concerning the propriety of Murrah remaining on the case. Katherine Hatch, "Murrah Role Questioned in Bid for School Review," *Daily Oklahoman,* Sept. 18, 1969, pp. 1–2.

51. Howard Davis, "Negro Group Joins School Opposition: Patrons Lose Intervenor Plea, Pledge Appeal," *Oklahoma City Times,* Aug. 14, 1969; Robert B. Allen, "In the Eye of a Storm: Busing Rulings Make Federal Judges Targets of Threats, Criticism, but They Won't Be Intimidated," *Orbit Magazine,* May 21, 1972, p. 18; David Fritze, "His Courage Counts," *Oklahoma Monthly,* Jan. 1978, p. 16; Davis, "Luther Bohanon," 51. In May 1974 a man telephoned Marie Bohanon and told her, "Your husband will be a dead man come Friday." When Bohanon arrived home that evening, he calmly reassured his wife, "If a fellow is gonna kill you, he's not going to tell you about it." Jim Henderson, "Bohanon Accepts Ill Will of Tough Rulings," *Tulsa World,* June 16, 1974, p. 1.

52. Jones, *From Brown to Boston,* 1860.

53. Henderson, "Bohanon Accepts," 1, 4; Paul English, "Anti-Busing Law Impossible Task?: Larry Derryberry's Dilemma," *Oklahoma Journal,* Feb. 8, 1970, pp. 1–2. It was not the first time that congressional action had been sought regarding Judge Bohanon. In 1966 his disputes with fellow judge Stephen Chandler led conservative Iowa representative H. R. Gross to call for a congressional investigation. Bohanon survived the attack, and no action was taken. Henderson, "Bohanon Accepts," 4. See also Hauan, *He Buys Organs,* 173–74.

54. Bryce Patterson, "Cluster Plan Author Says Judge Correct," *Daily Oklahoman,* Dec. 2, 1971.

55. Howard Davis, "Blacks Question Integration," *Oklahoma Journal*, Nov. 9, 1971, p. 1. By the time of the demonstrations of September 1972 described herein, James was at Sykes CME Church. Today he is pastor of Saint Mary's CME Church, acts as a special assistant to the bishop, and is a member of the Oklahoma City Council. Rev. Jonathan Bradshaw, pastor of Greater Cleaves Memorial CME Church in Oklahoma City, interview with author, May 6, 1991.

56. Davis, "Blacks Question," 2.

57. Franks and Lambert, *Legacy*, 87; *Dowell* v. *Board of Education*, 338 F. Supp. 1256, 1269 (W.D. Okl. 1972).

58. Davis, "Luther Bohanon," S1; "Busing Has Been a Necessary Evil," 27.

59. Bryce Patterson, "School System End Proposed," *Sunday Oklahoman*, Sept. 3, 1972, pp. 1, 2; "NAACP Hits Anti-Busing Leaders: Ministers' Help Asked," *Oklahoma City Times*, Sept. 2, 1972, p. 1; Mary Jo Nelson, "Ministers Seek Peace Before School Resumes," *Oklahoma City Times*, Sept. 4, 1972, p. 1.

60. "NAACP Hits," pp. 1–2; "They'll Tell the World," *Oklahoma City Times*, Sept. 6, 1972.

61. Jim Jackson and Bill Kronholm, "Attendance Picks Up As Race Tensions Ease," *Oklahoma City Times*, Sept. 5, 1972, pp. 1, 2.

62. Clipping in the private papers of Judge Bohanon.

63. Bohanon interview with author, Nov. 14, 1988.

64. "Time for Responsibility," *Oklahoma City Times*, Jan. 20, 1977, p. 44.

65. Order Terminating the Case, Jan. 18, 1977.

66. *Board of Education* v. *Dowell*, 89–1080—Opinion at 3 (S. Ct. January 15, 1991).

67. "Turning Back the Clock in the Oklahoma City Schools," *Equal Justice*, Autumn 1990, p. 7; Clara Luper interview with author, Feb. 25, 1991.

68. *Board of Education* v. *Dowell*, 89–1080—Dissent at 5–6; "Turning Back," 2; Chambers interview with author, Mar. 15, 1991.

69. *Swann* v. *Charlotte-Mecklenburg Board of Education*, 402 U.S. 1, 31–32 (1971); *Keyes* v. *School District No. 1*, 413 U.S. 189, 211 (1973).

70. Order, Judgment, Decree, cited in Bohanon, "Autobiography," X-23.

71. Bohanon interviews with author, Nov. 13–16, 1988; *Dowell v. Board of Education*, 890 F.2d 1483, 1491 (10th Cir. 1989).

72. Id. at 1490, 1504.

73. *Board of Education* v. *Dowell*, 89–1080—Opinion at 10; Chambers interview with author, Mar. 15, 1991.

74. *Board of Education* v. *Dowell*, 89–1080—Opinion at 10, 11–12.

75. *Board of Education* v. *Dowell*, 89–1080—Dissent at 14, 17. The civil rights movement and all that it spawned has been called the Second Reconstruction. See, for example, Marable, *Race*, 41; Garry Wills, *The Second Civil War: Arming for Armageddon*. When asked if the nation runs the risk of dismantling the Second Reconstruction prematurely in the same manner the first was abandoned, Jack Greenberg replied, "Yes, I think we do. We still have many, many, many years in front of us [before we can claim the process complete]." Greenberg interview with author, Feb. 6, 1991. In a separate interview, Julius Chambers, Greenberg's successor at the LDF, concurred. Chambers interview with author, Mar. 15, 1991.

By contrast, it is ironical that John Kennedy, hailed by Harry Golden as the nation's second great "Emancipator President" for his part in the Second Reconstruction, in his little-known sequel to *Profiles in Courage*, selected Andrew Johnson, the man largely responsible for dismantling the first Reconstruction, as one of the country's six bravest presidents. Johnson was selected by Kennedy for his foreign policy in affirming the Monroe Doctrine against France in Mexico. Harry Golden, *Mr. Kennedy and the Negroes*; Bill Davidson, *President Kennedy Selects Six Brave Presidents*. Davidson based the profiles on condensations of President Kennedy's words in discussions with him.

76. *Board of Education* v. *Dowell*, 89–1080—Dissent at 8, 18–19.

77. Patrick B. McGuigan, "Forced Busing: A Beginning and End," *Daily Oklahoman*, Jan. 16, 1991; Stephen Wermiel, "Supreme Court Eases Way for Schools in Busing Cases," *Wall Street Journal*, Jan. 16, 1991, p. A14.

78. Roberto Voci interview with author, Jan. 16, 1991; Wermiel, "Supreme Court," A14; Chambers interview with author, Mar. 16,

1991; Greenberg interview with author, Feb. 6, 1991; Linda Greenhouse, "Justices Rule Mandatory Busing May Go, Even If Races Stay Apart," *New York Times*, Jan. 16, 1991, p. B6.

79. *Board of Education* v. *Dowell*, 89–1080—Opinion at 11.

80. "Turning Back," pp. 2, 7; Chambers interview with author, Mar. 15, 1991.

81. "Turning Back," pp. 1–2.

82. Andrew Hacker, *Two Nations: Black and White, Separate, Hostile and Unequal*, 163.

83. John Perry, "City Schools Ruled Not Segregated," *Daily Oklahoman*, Nov. 8, 1991, p. 2; *Dowell* v. *Board of Education*, 778 F. Supp. 1144 at 1149 (W.D. Okl. 1977).

84. Id. at 1196.

85. Id. at 1196.

86. Perry, "City Schools," 1.

87. Ibid. David Duke, a former leader of the Ku Klux Klan, ran significant races for U.S. senator and governor in Louisiana. In 1992 he was also a candidate for the Republican nomination for president.

88. Order Denying Plaintiffs' Motion for Leave to File Motion for Relief from Judgment Pursuant to Fed. R. Civ. P. 60(b)(5) and (b)(6), filed Jan. 2, 1992, at 3; Bohanon correspondence with author, Jan. 27 and Feb. 7, 1992.

89. Order Denying Plaintiffs' Motion, at 15.

90. *Dowell*, 71 F.R.D. at 51.

91. Tom Boone, "Busing Support Plans Outlined," *Daily Oklahoman*, Sept. 3, 1972, p. 1. The statement by Stewart was made at a press conference to announce that the NAACP would assume a public leadership role in support of bussing and no longer limit itself to actions in the courts. The change in policy came at the recommendation of NAACP national executive secretary Roy Wilkins.

92. Bohanon interview with author, Apr. 5, 1991.

V. THE PRISON CASE

1. William A. Fletcher, "The Discretionary Constitution: Institutional Remedies and Judicial Legitimacy," 91 Yale L. J. 635 at 684 (1982).

2. Ibid.; Theodore Eisenberg and Stephen C. Yeazell, "The Ordi-

nary and the Extraordinary in Institutional Litigation," 93 Harv. L. Rev. 465 (1980).

3. Eisenberg and Yeazell, "Ordinary," 516.

4. See Fletcher, "Discretionary Constitution."

5. "Judges Overstep Power," *Oklahoma City Times*, Nov. 6, 1981. Edward L. Gaylord had succeeded to ownership of the Oklahoma Publishing Company upon the death of his father in 1974.

6. "McAlester Called Shameful: Black Convict Wins Suit Against State Prison," *Tulsa Tribune*, Mar. 16, 1974, p. 1.

7. Frosty Troy transcript of radio commentary, May 30, 1977, in private papers of Judge Bohanon; Frosty Troy, "Bohanonism," *Oklahoma Observer*, July 25, 1979; "Bohanon Gets Tough," *Tulsa Daily World*, June 1, 1974, p. 6A; Luther Lee Bohanon, "The Autobiography of Judge Luther L. Bohanon," unpublished manuscript, XI-1; Frosty Troy, "Oklahoman of the Year: Judge Luther Bohanon," *Oklahoma Observer*, Jan. 25, 1984, p. 1.

8. *Sunday Oklahoman*, July 28, 1974, p. 10.

9. Bohanon to author, Oct. 14, 1991.

10. Gary Minnich, "Bohanon Orders Prison Reforms," *Oklahoma Journal*, Mar. 16, 1974, p. 1.

11. "McAlester Called," 1.

12. Minnich, "Bohanon Orders," 1; Elizabeth Alexander, "The New Prison Administrators and the Court: New Directions in Prison Law," 56 Tex. L. Rev. 963 at.997 (1978).

13. *Battle* v. *Anderson*, 376 F. Supp. 402, 428 (E.D. Okl. 1974); Jim Henderson, "Bohanon Accepts Ill Will of Tough Rulings," *Tulsa World*, June 16, 1974, p. 4.

14. "Defusing the Time Bomb," *Tulsa Tribune*, June 3, 1974; "Bohanon Gets Tough," 6A.

15. "Bohanon's Right Answer," *Tulsa World*, Dec. 10, 1980, p. 6A.

16. Gail Abney, "Prison Ruling to Be Obeyed: Compliance Vowed," *Daily Oklahoman*, June 4, 1974, p. 2. With regard to chemical agents, the order read:

The unjustified use of chemical agents against inmates is prohibited. They shall not be used against individual inmates, or against small groups of them, except as authorized by the policy statement of the Oklahoma State Department of Corrections dated January 3, 1973. To support the use of this form of physical force, the requirement of that policy statement that there be an actual and imminent threat of bodily harm must be present. Chemical agents may also be used to quell an actual or incipient riot involving a large number of unconfined inmates, where there is present an actual and imminent threat of serious damage to or the destruction of property which is substantial in quantity and/or value. They may also be used to thwart the imminent escape of an inmate or inmates."

17. Ibid., 2; "McAlester Called," 1.

18. Bohanon, "Autobiography," XI-14.

19. Frosty Troy transcript of radio commentary, May 31, 1977, in private papers of Judge Bohanon.

20. *Battle* v. *Anderson*, 447 F. Supp. 516, 517 (E.D. Okl. 1977).

21. Id. at 525.

22. In order to put the court's order in perspective, it is useful to note that the area of a king-size bed is about fifty-two square feet.

23. *Battle* v. *Anderson*, 457 F. Supp. 719, 740 (E.D. Okl. 1978).

24. Gene Triplett, "Prison Reform Haste Ordered, Strict Timetable Set: Bohanon Quotes Scripture," *Oklahoma Journal*, Sept. 12, 1978, p. 2.

25. Jim Young, "Benton Says Odds Poor on Winning Prison Order Appeal: Cost of Reforms Estimated at $30 Million to $50 Million," *Oklahoma City Times*, Sept. 12, 1978, p. 1.

26. Terry Maxon, "State Faces Big Spending for Prisons," *Oklahoma Journal*, Sept. 12, 1978, p. 2.

27. Ibid.; Young, "Benton Says," 2.

28. "Bohanon's Right," 6A.

29. "Better Late Than Never," *Daily Oklahoman*, May 2, 1982.

30. *Rhodes* v. *Chapman*, 452 U.S. 337 (1981).

31. Bohanon, "Autobiography," XI-17.

32. "Judge Orders White Officials for 2 Schools: Bohanon Oks Board's Pupil Assignments" and "Prison Ruling to Be Obeyed: Compliance Vowed," *Daily Oklahoman*, June 4, 1974, p. 1; William C. Kellough, "Power and Politics of the Oklahoma Federal Court," *Chronicles of Oklahoma*, Summer 1987, p. 203; Stella Roberts, "Supreme Court May Rule on Mixing," *Tampa Tribune*, Dec. 7, 1969.

33. Bohanon interview with author, Nov. 14, 1988.

34. Ibid.; Roberts, "Supreme Court"; Clara Luper, *Behold the*

Walls, 244. One cannot help but wonder if Luper has changed her estimation in the wake of the latest *Dowell* decision.

35. Bohanon interview with author, Nov. 13, 1988.

36. Sheryl McCarthy, "Old Wrongs Don't Make Thomas Right," *New York Newsday*, July 3, 1991, pp. 7, 17; Bohanon interview with author, July 31, 1991. Although Judge Bohanon voiced no opinion about the qualifications of Judge Thomas for the nation's highest court, it being improper for a sitting judge to do so, after extensive conversations it is clear to me that it is highly unlikely that he favored the appointment. Judge Bohanon believes that no one is qualified to sit on the federal bench unless he or she believes in all the rights guaranteed by the Constitution. For Judge Bohanon, that includes the right to privacy articulated by *Roe* v. *Wade*.

VI. THE NATIVE AMERICAN LAND CASE

1. *United States* v. *Texas*, 162 U.S. 1 (1896); *Choctaw Nation* v. *Cherokee Nation*, 393 F. Supp. 224 (E.D. Okl. 1975). *Rhode Island* v. *Massachusetts*, 12 Pet. 657; *New Jersey* v. *New York*, 5 Pet. 284; *Missouri* v. *Iowa*, 7 How. 660; *Florida* v. *Georgia*, 17 How. 478; *Alabama* v. *Georgia*, 23 How. 505; *Virginia* v. *West Virginia*, 11 Wall. 39; and *Indiana* v. *Kentucky*, 136 U.S. 479, were all suits brought for judicial determination of disputed boundaries.

2. Anne Hodges Morgan, *Robert S. Kerr: The Senate Years*, 140–41.

3. Martin Hauan, *He Buys Organs for Churches, Pianos for Bawdy Houses*, 149.

4. Governor Edmondson's remark in a memorial address for Kerr, quoted in Morgan, *Kerr*, 142–43; Douglas's comment in ibid., 150.

5. David R. Morgan; Robert E. England; and George G. Humphreys, *Oklahoma Politics and Policies: Governing the Sooner State*, 28; Theodore Sorensen, *The Kennedy Legacy*, 250. Sorensen, however, misremembers what river Kerr was trying to develop, referring mistakenly to the Red River.

6. Morgan, *Kerr*, 143.

7. Hauan, *He Buys Organs*, 161.

8. *Lawton Constitution–Morning Press*, September 23, 1962; Morgan, *Kerr*, 174.

9. Bohanon to author, Apr. 4, 1989; *Choctaw Nation* v. *Oklahoma*, 397 U.S. 620, 621 (1970).

10. Id. at 622.

11. *Choctaw Nation* v. *Cherokee Nation*, 393 F. Supp. at 226.

12. Bohanon to author, Apr. 4, 1989; Bohanon interview with author, Apr. 8, 1989. The trial in *Battle* was set for six weeks later on Mar. 14, 1974.

13. Bohanon to author, Apr. 4, 1989.

14. *Cherokee Nation* v. *Georgia*, 5 Pet. 1 (1831); *Worcester* v. *Georgia*, 6 Pet. 515 (1832).

15. Billy M. Jones and Odie B. Faulk, *Cherokees: An Illustrated History*, 62. For an interesting, albeit fictionalized, account of Cherokee history during this era by a person of Indian descent, Everett O. Campbell, *The Eagle Flies at Dawn: A Saga of the Cherokee People.*

16. See generally, *Choctaw Nation* v. *Cherokee Nation*, 393 F. Supp. 224.

17. Bohanon to author, Apr. 4, 1989; *Choctaw Nation* v. *Oklahoma*, 397 U.S. at 621; *Choctaw Nation* v. *Cherokee Nation*, 393 F. Supp. at 232–33.

18. *Choctaw Nation* v. *Oklahoma*, 397 U.S. at 643 (Douglas, J. concurring).

VII. THE LAETRILE CASE

1. *Rutherford* v. *United States*, 438 F. Supp. 1287, 1296 (W.D. Okl. 1977); "Bohanon: Laetrile Legal," *Oklahoma Journal*, Dec. 6, 1977, p. 1.

2. *United States* v. *Rutherford*, 442 U.S. 544, 548 (1979).

3. Bohanon interview with author, Nov. 13, 1988; *Rutherford* v. *United States*, 399 F. Supp. 1208, 1211 (W.D. Okl. 1975).

4. *Rutherford*, 399 F. Supp. at 1211–12.

5. Id. at 1213; *Rutherford* v. *United States*, 542 F.2d 1137, 1139 (10th Cir. 1976).

6. *Rutherford*, 542 F.2d at 1140, 1144.

7. *Rutherford* v. *United States*, 424 F. Supp. 105, 107 (W.D. Okl. 1977).

8. *Rutherford* v. *United States*, 429 F. Supp. 506, 508 (W.D. Okl. 1977).

9. Id. at 509.

10. *Rutherford* v. *United States*, 582 F.2d 1234, 1236 (10th Cir. 1978).

11. *Rutherford*, 438 F. Supp. at 1300, 1301.

12. Id. at 1300.

13. *Rutherford*, 442 U.S. at 555–56, 558, 559.

14. *Rutherford*, 438 F. Supp. at 1301.

15. *Rutherford* v. *United States*, 616 F.2d 455, 457 (10th Cir. 1980); *Rutherford* v. *United States*, 449 U.S. 937 (1980).

16. *Rutherford* v. *United States*, 806 F.2d 1455 (10th Cir. 1986). A writ of mandamus is an extraordinary action and traditionally has been used in response to an abuse of judicial power. Thus, where a district court judge refuses to take some action he or she is required to take or takes an action outside the scope of his or her power, mandamus will lie, and a superior court will direct compliance with its edict.

17. David Fritze, "His Courage Counts," *Oklahoma Monthly*, Jan. 1978, p. 21; Bohanon interviews with author, Nov. 13–14, 1988.

18. Bohanon interview with author, Nov. 13, 1988.

19. Bohanon interview with author, Nov. 13, 1988. For an excellent account of the turbulent history of the *Roe* case, see Marian Faux, *Roe v. Wade*.

20. William Schneider, "Playing Games with the Court," *Los Angeles Times*, July 7, 1991, pp. M1, M6.

21. Bohanon interview with author, Nov. 13, 1988.

22. Fritze, "His Courage Counts," 21.

EPILOGUE

1. Alfred Silver, *Where the Ghost Horse Runs*, 411; Peter C. Newman, *Caesars of the Wilderness*, xii. Bert Barefoot, Jr., was also kind enough to provide his assessment of Judge Bohanon in a manuscript prepared as a foreword for an earlier version of this work. All quotes from him come from that brief piece.

2. Stella Roberts, "Supreme Court May Rule on Mixing," *Tampa Tribune*, Dec. 7, 1969; Bohanon interviews with author, Nov. 13–16, 1988. It is characteristic of Judge Bohanon that in conversation he consistently seeks to diminish the significance of any case in which he was reversed. An example of this is the fact that during the preparation of this book he asked that a particular case

be deleted from the table of cases contained in the Appendix, citing as his reason that the case was not significant and that he had been reversed in his decision in it. After some discussion, the case remained on the list. See also, "Justice at Snail's Pace," *Sunday Oklahoman*, Sept. 25, 1988, p. 12, dealing with the judge's handling of a case involving bingo on the tribal land of the Potawatomi Indians.

As an example of Bohanon's apolitical libertarianism, he admits that until he handled the *Dowell* case he had never been particularly sensitive to the plight of African-Americans. Likewise, he refused to see Bobby Battle when the latter approached him.

3. Barefoot manuscript.

4. Archibald Cox, *The Court and the Constitution*, 26.

5. Jim Henderson, "Bohanon Accepts Ill Will of Tough Rulings," *Tulsa World*, June 16, 1974, p. 4.

The "religious theory" of the law refers to the school of thought that holds that the law has a separate existence. The "law" is seen as a body of rules, "the correct application of which could be discovered in any given situation by logical deduction from the body of reports of previous decisions." Cox, *Court and Constitution*, 181. For a fuller discussion of the theory, see chapter 2, above. The term was coined, as far as I know, by attorney Susanna Shields to contrast its proponents with those of the legal realist school.

6. Cox, *Court and Constitution*, 26, 376.

Bibliography

MEMOIRS, MANUSCRIPTS, AND INTERVIEWS

Barefoot, Bert, Jr. Manuscript prepared as foreword for earlier version of this book.

Berry, William A. Manuscript prepared as foreword for earlier version of this book.

Bohanon, Luther Lee. "The Autobiography of Judge Luther L. Bohanon." Manuscript made available to author by Judge Bohanon, 1988.

———. "A Word From the Wise Did Not Work." Unpublished article.

———. *Opinions of the Honorable Luther L. Bohanon, Judge, United States District Court.* 4 vols. Saint Paul, Minn.: West Publishing Co., 1974–86. Compilation of certain published opinions of Judge Bohanon (1970–86), prepared by legal publisher as gift for the judge.

———. Personal interviews and correspondence with the author, 1988–92.

———. Private papers made available to the author by Judge Bohanon. Include portions of the judge's correspondence, personal files, notes, photographs, unpublished decisions, and articles.

———. Transcript of the swearing in and robing of Honorable Luther L. Bohanon as judge of the United States District Court for the Western, Northern, and Eastern Districts of the State of Oklahoma, United States Courthouse, Oklahoma City, Okla., Sept. 11, 1961.

Bradshaw, Jonathan. Telephone interview with author, Oklahoma City, May 6, 1991.

Chambers, Julius. Interview with author, New York City, Mar. 15, 1991.

"Commemorative Devotion: University of Oklahoma College of Law, Class of 1927, in Honor of Educators Who Give Man His Tomorrow." Inscription on base of statue of Dean Julien C. Monnet, University of Oklahoma Law Center, Norman.

Corn, N. S. Transcript of sworn statement, Medical Center for Federal Prisoners, Springfield, Mo., Dec. 9, 1964.

Greenberg, Jack. Interview with author, New York City, Feb. 6, 1991.

Hauan, Martin. *He Buys Organs for Churches, Pianos for Bawdy Houses.* Oklahoma City: Midwest Political Publications, 1976.

————. *How to Win Elections Without Hardly Cheatin' At All.* Oklahoma City: Midwest Political Publications, 1983.

Kennedy, Robert. Transcript of oral history interviews by Anthony Lewis, John F. Kennedy Library, Boston, Mass.

Luper, Clara. *Behold the Walls.* Oklahoma City: Jim Wire, 1979. Privately printed in a small run, it was made available to the author by Mrs. Luper.

————. Telephone interview with author, Feb. 25, 1991.

Ray, Susan Heinze. Telephone interviews with author, Oklahoma City, 1988–92.

Troy, Frosty. "Frosty Troy Commentary." Transcripts of radio commentaries for May 30 and 31, 1977, in private papers of Judge Bohanon.

U.S. District Court. Unpublished history of the federal district court of Oklahoma prepared by and for the court.

Voci, Roberto. Telephone interview with author, Norman, Okla., Jan. 16, 1991.

BOOKS

Abernathy, Ralph David. *And the Walls Came Tumbling Down.* New York: Harper & Row, 1989.

Adams, James Luther. *An Examined Faith.* Ed. with intro. by George K. Beach. Boston: Beacon Press, 1991.

Alexander, Charles C. *The Ku Klux Klan in the Southwest.* Lexington: University of Kentucky Press, 1965.

Baker, Liva. *The Justice from Beacon Hill: The Life and Times of Oliver Wendell Holmes.* New York: Harper-Collins Publishers, 1991.

Barnes, Catherine A. *Journey from Jim Crow: The Desegregation of Southern Transit.* New York: Columbia University Press, 1983.

Bell, Derrick. *And We Are Not Saved: The Elusive Quest for Racial Justice.* New York: Basic Books, 1987.

———. *Faces at the Bottom of the Well: The Permanence of Racism.* New York: Basic Books, 1992.

Bennett, Lerone, Jr. *Before the Mayflower: A History of Black America.* 5th rev. ed. New York: Penguin Books, 1982.

Blackstone, William. *Commentaries on the Laws of England.* 4 vols. Oxford: Clarendon Press, 1765–69.

Branch, Taylor. *Parting the Waters: America in the King Years, 1954–1963.* New York: Simon & Schuster, 1988.

Bryant, Keith L., Jr. *Alfalfa Bill Murray.* Norman: University of Oklahoma Press, 1968.

Burbank, Garin. *When Farmers Voted Red: The Gospel of Socialism in the Oklahoma Countryside, 1910–1924.* Westport, Conn.: Greenwood Press, 1976.

Campbell, Everett O. *The Eagle Flies at Dawn: A Saga of the Cherokee People.* New York: Vantage Press, 1989.

Chapman, Berlin Basil. *The Otoes and Missourias: A Study of Indian Removal and the Legal Aftermath.* Oklahoma City: Times Journal Publishing Company, 1965.

Clifford, Clark. *Counsel to the President.* New York: Random House, 1991.

Cluster, Dick, ed. *They Should Have Served That Cup of Coffee.* Boston: South End Press, 1979.

Collier, John. *Indians of the Americas.* New York: W. W. Norton & Company, 1947.

Cone, James H. *Malcolm & Martin & America: A Dream or a Nightmare.* Maryknoll, N.Y.: Orbis Books, 1991.

Countryman, Vern, ed. *The Douglas Opinions.* New York: Random House, 1977.

Cox, Archibald. *The Court and the Constitution.* Boston: Houghton Mifflin Company, 1987.

Cross, George Lynn. *Blacks in White Colleges: Oklahoma's Landmark Cases.* Norman: University of Oklahoma Press, 1975.

———. *Professors, Presidents, and Politicians: Civil Rights and the University of Oklahoma, 1890–1968.* Norman: University of Oklahoma Press, 1981.

Cruse, Harold. *Plural but Equal.* New York: William Morrow and Company, 1987.

Dallek, Robert. *Lone Star Rising: Lyndon Johnson and His Times 1908–1960.* New York: Oxford University Press, 1991.

Davidson, Bill. *President Kennedy Selects Six Brave Presidents.* New York: Harper & Row, Publishers, 1962.

Davis, John H. *The Kennedys: Dynasty and Disaster, 1848–1983.* New York: McGraw-Hill Book Company, 1984.

Davis, Michael D., and Hunter R. Clark. *Thurgood Marshall: Warrior at the Bar, Rebel on the Bench.* New York: Birch Lane Press, 1992.

Duroselle, Jean-Baptiste. *La Décadence: 1932–1939.* Paris: Imprimerie Nationale, 1979.

Ellison, Ralph. *Going to the Territory.* New York: Random House, 1986.

Faux, Marian. *Roe v. Wade.* New York: Macmillan, 1988.

Ford, Paul L., ed. *The Writings of Thomas Jefferson.* New York: Putnam, 1892–1899.

Franks, Kenny A., and Paul F. Lambert. *The Legacy of Dean Julien C. Monnet: Judge Luther Bohanon and the Deseg-*

regation of Oklahoma City's Public Schools. Muskogee, Okla.: Western Heritage Books, 1984.

Garrow, David J. *Bearing the Cross: Martin Luther King, Jr., and the Southern Christian Leadership Conference.* New York: William Morrow and Company, 1986.

Ginger, Ray. *Eugene V. Debs: Making of an American Radical.* 1962 ed. New York: Collier Books, 1962.

Goble, Danney. *Progressive Oklahoma: The Making of a New Kind of State.* Norman: University of Oklahoma Press, 1980.

Golden, Harry. *Mr. Kennedy and the Negroes.* Cleveland: World Publishing Company, 1964.

——. *Only in America.* Cleveland: World Publishing Company, 1958.

Goldman, Roger, and David Gallen. *Thurgood Marshall: Justice for All.* New York: Carroll & Graf Publishers, 1992.

Green, James R. *Grass-Roots Socialism: Radical Movements in the Southwest, 1895–1943.* Baton Rouge: Louisiana State University Press, 1978.

Guthman, Edwin O., and Jeffrey Schulman, eds. *Robert Kennedy in His Own Words.* New York: Bantam Books, 1988.

Hacker, Andrew. *Two Nations: Black and White, Separate, Hostile and Unequal.* New York: Charles Scribner's Sons, 1992.

Hamilton, Charles V. *The Bench and the Ballot: Southern Federal Judges and Black Voters.* New York: Oxford University Press, 1973.

Harding, Vincent. *There Is a River: The Black Struggle for Freedom in America.* New York: Harcourt Brace Jovanovich, 1981.

Harlow, Rex. *Oklahoma Leaders.* Oklahoma City: Harlow Publishing Company, 1928.

Holmes, Oliver Wendell, Jr. *The Common Law & Other Writings.* Birmingham: The Legal Classics Library, 1982.

Hudson, William. *A Treatise of the Court of Star Chamber.* Ed. Francis Hargrave. Birmingham: The Legal Classics Library, 1986.

Hughes, Charles Evans. *The Autobiographical Notes of Charles Evans Hughes.* Ed. David Danelski and Joseph Tulchin. Cambridge: Harvard University Press, 1973.

Jackson, Kenneth T. *The Ku Klux Klan in the City, 1915–1930.* New York: Oxford University Press, 1967.

Jones, Billy M., and Odie B. Faulk, *Cherokees: An Illustrated History.* Muskogee, Okla.: The Five Civilized Tribes Museum, 1984.

Jones, Leon. *From Brown to Boston: Desegregation in Education, 1954–1974,* Vol. II. *Legal Cases and Indexes.* Metuchen, N.J.: The Scarecrow Press, 1979.

Kent, James. *Commentaries on American Law.* 4 vols. New York: O. Halsted, 1826–30.

Kluger, Richard. *Simple Justice.* New York: Alfred A. Knopf, 1976.

Levitan, Sar A.; William B. Johnston; and Robert Taggart. *Still a Dream: The Changing Status of Blacks Since 1960.* Cambridge: Harvard University Press, 1975.

McCarthy, Eugene. *Up 'Til Now.* New York: Harcourt Brace Jovanovich, 1987.

Marable, Manning. *Race, Reform and Rebellion: The Second Reconstruction in Black America, 1945–1982.* Jackson: University Press of Mississippi, 1984.

Mathews, John Joseph. *Life and Death of an Oilman: the Career of E. W. Marland.* Norman: University of Oklahoma Press, 1951.

Mooney, Booth. *LBJ: An Irreverent Chronicle.* New York: Thomas Y. Crowell Company, 1976.

Morgan, Anne Hodges. *Robert S. Kerr: The Senate Years.* Norman: University of Oklahoma Press, 1977.

Morgan, David R.; Robert E. England; and George G. Humphreys. *Oklahoma Politics and Policies: Governing the Sooner State.* Lincoln: University of Nebraska Press, 1991.

Morris, Aldon D. *The Origins of the Civil Rights Movement: Black Communities Organizing for Change.* New York: The Free Press, 1984.

Morris, John W.; Charles R. Goins; and Edwin C. McReynolds. *Historical Atlas of Oklahoma.* 2d ed. Norman: University of Oklahoma Press, 1976.

Newman, Peter C. *Caesars of the Wilderness.* Markham, Ont.: Viking, 1987.

Novick, Sheldon M. *Honorable Justice: The Life of Oliver Wendell Holmes.* Boston: Little, Brown and Company, 1989.

Peltason, J. W. *Fifty-eight Lonely Men: Southern Federal Judges and School Desegregation.* New York: Harcourt, Brace & World, 1961.

Raines, Howell. *My Soul Is Rested.* New York: G. P. Putnam & Sons, 1977.

Randel, William Peirce. *The Ku Klux Klan: A Century of Infamy.* Philadelphia: Chilton Books, 1965.

Salinger, Pierre. *With Kennedy.* Garden City, N.Y.: Doubleday & Company, 1966.

Scales, James R., and Danney Goble. *Oklahoma Politics: A History.* Norman: University of Oklahoma Press, 1982.

Schlesinger, Arthur M., Jr. *Robert Kennedy and His Times.* Boston: Houghton Mifflin Company, 1978.

Seeger, Pete, and Bob Reiser. *Everybody Says Freedom.* New York: W. W. Norton & Company, 1989.

Silver, Alfred. *Where the Ghost Horse Runs.* New York: Ballantine Books, 1991.

Sorensen, Theodore C. *The Kennedy Legacy.* New York: Macmillan, 1969.

Strickland, Rennard. *Fire and the Spirits: Cherokee Law from Clan to Court.* Norman: University of Oklahoma Press, 1975.

Teall, Kaye M. *Black History in Oklahoma: A Resource Book.* Oklahoma City: Title III, ESEA, Oklahoma City Public Schools, 1971.

Thoburn, Joseph B., and Muriel H. Wright. *Oklahoma: A History.* 4 vols. New York: Lewis Historical Publishing Company, 1929.

Thompson, John. *Closing the Frontier: Radical Response in Oklahoma, 1889–1923.* Norman: University of Oklahoma Press, 1986.

Voigt, Edwin, et al., eds. *The Book of Hymns.* Nashville: United Methodist Publishing House, 1964.

Washburn, Wilcomb E. *Red Man's Land / White Man's Law: A Study of the Past and Present Status of the American Indian.* New York: Charles Scribner's Sons, 1971.

Washington, James M., ed. *A Testament of Hope: The Essential Writings of Martin Luther King, Jr.* San Francisco: Harper & Row, Publishers, 1986.

Watkins, T. H. *Righteous Pilgrim: The Life and Times of Harold L. Ickes, 1874–1952.* New York: Henry Holt and Company, 1990.

Weisbrot, Robert. *Freedom Bound: A History of America's Civil Rights Movement.* New York: W. W. Norton and Company, 1990.

White, Anne Terry. *Eugene Debs: American Socialist.* New York: Lawrence Hill and Company, 1974.

Who's Who in America. Chicago: Marquis, 1980.

Wills, Garry. *The Second Civil War.* New York: New American Library, 1968.

Woodward, C. Vann. *The Strange Career of Jim Crow.* 3d rev. ed. New York: Oxford University Press, 1974.

Young, Robert J. *In Command of France.* Cambridge: Harvard University Press, 1978.

ARTICLES

Alexander, Elizabeth. "The New Prison Administrators and the Court: New Directions in Prison Law." 56 Tex. L. Rev. 963 (1978).

Allen, Robert B. "In the Eye of a Storm: Busing Rulings Make Federal Judges Targets of Threats, Criticism, but They Won't Be Intimidated." *Orbit Magazine,* May 21, 1972.

Bliven, Naomi. "Say Not the Struggle Naught Availeth." *New Yorker,* Jan. 28, 1991.

Boulton, Scot W. "Desegregation of the Oklahoma City School System." *Chronicles of Oklahoma,* Summer 1980.

Eisenberg, Theodore, and Stephen C. Yeazell. "The Ordinary and the Extraordinary in Institutional Litigation." 93 Harv. L. Rev. 465 (1980).

Ervin, Sam, Jr. "Separation of Powers, Judicial Independence." 35 Law and Contemp. Probl. 108 (1970).

Fletcher, William A. "The Discretionary Constitution: Institutional Remedies and Judicial Legitimacy." 91 Yale L. J. 635 (1982).

Frazier, Ruth. "Covered Wagons of '72." *Orbit Magazine,* Dec. 24, 1972.

Fritze, David. "His Courage Counts." *Oklahoma Monthly,* Jan. 1978.

Gibbs, Nancy. "Filling a Legal Giant's Shoes." *Time,* July 8, 1991.

Graves, Carl R. "The Right to be Served: Oklahoma City's Lunch Counter Sit-ins, 1958–1964." *Chronicles of Oklahoma,* Summer 1981.

Hand, Learned. "Mr. Justice Cardozo." 52 Harv. L. Rev. 361 (1939).

Kellough, William C. "Power and Politics of the Oklahoma Federal Court." *Chronicles of Oklahoma,* Summer 1987.

Lacayo, Richard. "A Lawyer Who Changed America." *Time,* July 8, 1991.

McMichael, Tom, and Keith Coplin. "Luther Bohanon." *Logos,* 1974.

"Turning Back the Clock in the Oklahoma City Schools." *Equal Justice,* Autumn 1990.

DISSERTATIONS

Saxe, Allan. "Protest and Reform: The Desegregation of Oklahoma City." Ph.D. diss., University of Oklahoma, 1969.

Stephens, Carol Louise. "The Urban League of Oklahoma City Oklahoma." Ph.D. diss., University of Oklahoma, 1957.

NEWSPAPERS

Boston Globe
Daily Oklahoman (Oklahoma City)
Journal Record (Oklahoma City)
Lawton Constitution–Morning Press
Los Angeles Times
New York Newsday
New York Times
Norman Transcript
Oklahoma: Official Publication of the Oklahoma City Chamber of Commerce
Oklahoma City Times
Oklahoma Journal (Oklahoma City)
Oklahoma Observer (Oklahoma City)
San Diego Union
Saturday Oklahoman & Times (Oklahoma City; joint Saturday edition)
Seminole Producer
Syracuse Herald-Journal
Tampa Tribune
Tulsa Daily World
Tulsa Tribune
Wall Street Journal

Index

Abernathy, Ralph, 184
Adams, Lynn, 44
African-Americans, and civil
 rights, 10–12, 71–116, 126,
 181–90
Albert, Carl, 142
Alexander, Martin S., 174
American Baptist Home Mis-
 sionary Society, 77
American Bar Association
 (ABA), 57–58, 61, 62; rating of
 Bohanon, 58, 63, 65
American Civil Liberties Union
 (ACLU), 111, 121, 123, 125,
 129, 131, 134–35
American College of Law Asso-
 ciation, 29–30
American Indian Defense Asso-
 ciation, 46
American Indian land claims,
 45–50, 178–79, 193–94;
 Cherokee Nation v. *United
 States*, 143, 194; Choctaw-
 Chickasaw-Cherokee Bound-
 ary Dispute Act, 142; *Choc-
 taw Nation* v. *Cherokee
 Nation*, 138, 141–44; *Otoe &
 Missouria* v. *United States*,
 45–50, 178–79

American Indians, 18, 72, 122,
 182, 185; Cherokee, 5, 184,
 194; Choctaw, 17, 18, 21, 74;
 Otoes and Missourias, 45–50,
 142. *See also* American In-
 dian land claims
American Inns of Court, 69–70
American Medical Association,
 147
American Party, 96–97
Amygdalin. *See* Laetrile
Anderson, Park, 121, 124
Arkansas River and navigation
 project, 48, 139–41, 143

Baker, Bobby, 60
Bane, Mary, 125–26
Bankwitz, Philip C. F., 173
Barefoot, Bert, Jr., 44, 49, 54,
 157, 158, 195, 196
Barrett, James, 135
Battle, Bobby, 116, 120, 121,
 125, 136, 196
Battle v. *Anderson*, 11, 117,
 118, 120–37, 142, 176,
 190–93
Bell, Derrick, 7, 78, 83–84, 174,
 181, 183, 185
Benton, Ned, 132, 133

Berry, William A., 51–52, 179
Bishop, Homer, 35, 36
Black Dispatch, 77, 78
Blackmun, Justice Harry, 109
Black Voices, 185
Bliven, Naomi, 46, 178
Bohanon, Artelia Hickman, 16, 17
Bohanon, Lucy Cain Cox, 17, 19–20, 23
Bohanon, Luther Lee: ancestry, 16; appointment as judge, 43, 50, 55–64; Army Air Corps, 43–44; assistant county attorney, 35–36; birth, 17; childhood, 17–24, 157; courtroom conduct, 6–67, 70, 181; credo, 9, 54; education, 18, 21–34; family life, 18–23; and institutional cases, 7–9, 118–19; legal practice, 36–38, 41, 44, 54; and privacy issues, 9, 151–56, 193; religious formation, 11, 19, 32–33, 46, 68; retirement, 8, 11; *Selected Investments* case, 50–53, 116; and sex discrimination, 9, 175; siblings, 14–25, 176
Bohanon, Marie, 38, 43, 96, 187
Bohanon, William, 16–18, 20, 23, 26–28, 176
Boren, David, 12, 127, 129, 132, 133, 175–76
Bork, Robert, 5
Brennan, Justice William, 95
Briggs v. *Elliot*, 4, 84, 174
Brown v. *Board of Education of Topeka, Kansas*, 3–4, 6–7, 12, 80–84, 87, 90, 93, 99, 109–11, 174, 184

Bullock, Louis, 134–35
Bullock, W. A., 79
Bureau of Indian Affairs (BIA), 45, 46, 48, 49
Busby, Oral, 35
Byrd, Harry, 60
Byrd, Janell, 111, 114, 116

Calhoun, John C., 139
Cape Kennedy, Fla., 91
Cardozo, Benjamin, 3, 8, 174
Carroll, Hugh, 51, 52
Chambers, Julius, 108, 111, 182, 189, 190
Cherokee Nation v. *United States*. *See* American Indian land claims
Choctaw-Chickasaw-Cherokee Boundary Dispute Act. *See* American Indian land claims
Choctaw Nation v. *Cherokee Nation*. *See* American Indian land claims
Choctaw Nation v. *Oklahoma*. *See* American Indian land claims
Clifford, Clark, 59
Collier, John, 45, 46, 178
Countryman, Vern, 173
Cox, Archibald, 5, 14, 15, 159, 174–76, 196
Cox, William H., 180
Cross, George Lynn, 77, 79–80, 182–84
Curtis Act, 17

Daugherty, Fred, 88, 142, 147, 184
Davis, Justice David, 8, 175
Derryberry, Larry, 97, 127, 132, 187

Desegregation: housing, 9, 89,
    119, 175, 186; lunch counter,
    84–86, 185–86; National
    Guard, 9, 119, 175; Okla-
    homa background, 72–79;
    school, 4, 7, 9–11, 72, 78–84,
    86–116, 142, 181–90
Doe v. *Bolton*, 146
Douglas, Paul, 140
Douglas, Justice William O.,
    144, 146, 155
Dowell v. *Board of Education*,
    7, 10–11, 71, 72, 75, 86–116,
    136, 142, 181–90, 194
Dowell, Alonzo L., 10, 72,
    86–88, 99
Dowell, Robert, 10, 72, 86, 87,
    89, 97, 104, 107, 108, 112,
    114, 115
Doyle, William, 135
Dred Scott v. *Sandford*, 82
Duke, David, 114, 190
Dunjee, John, 77
Dunjee, Roscoe, 77–80, 85, 183,
    185

Eastland, James O., 180
Edmondson, Ed, 132
Edmondson, J. Howard, 61, 193
Eisenberg, Theodore, 118, 190,
    191
Ellison, Ralph, 185
Enabling Act, 74
Ervin, Sam, 13, 176

Fabian, Judith, 175
Finger, John, 97–100, 102, 103,
    111, 116
Fisher, Ada Lois Sipuel, 79–80
Food, Drug, and Cosmetics Act,
    151, 154

Food and Drug Administration
    (FDA), 9, 147–51, 153–55
Franklin, Neal D., 44

Gary, Raymond, 82
Gaylord, Edward King ("E. K.")
    (father), 90–91, 191
Gaylord, Edward L. (son), 92,
    102, 119, 134, 191
Goble, Danney, 73, 182
Golden, Harry, 86, 186, 189
Gore, Thomas Pryor, 40, 41,
    178
Graves, Carl, 85, 86, 185, 186
Green, John, 87
Greenberg, Jack, 72, 111, 182,
    189, 190
Grider, John, 128
Guinn v. *United States*, 75–77,
    183

Hall, Amos, 80
Hall, David, 127
Hamilton, Bill, 74
Hand, Learned, 3, 6, 8, 158, 159,
    174
Hauan, Martin, 6, 56, 176,
    179–81, 193
Hawks, Rex, 61–62
Hill, Delmas C., 7
Hill, Virgil, 93
Hinds, H. I., 61
Hodgins, Amy, 132
Hollins v. *Oklahoma*, 78
Holmes, Justice Oliver
    Wendell, 33, 177
Houston, Sam, 139
Howard, Gene, 133
Hughes, Chief Justice Charles
    Evans, 33, 177
Hunter, Lettie Ruth, 111–12

Huxman, Walter, 6, 7
Hyde, Herbert K., 48

Ickes, Harold, 45–46, 178
Indian Claims Commission Act
  of 1946, 49

Jackson, Andrew, 143, 174
James, Goree, 98, 100–101, 188
Jefferson, Thomas, 14
Johnson, Lyndon Baines, 56, 57,
  59, 60, 179
Johnson v. Avery, 117
Judiciary, independence of,
  12–14, 175–76

Katz Drugstore, 85
Kempton, Murray, 12–13, 176
Kennedy, John F., 10, 55–62, 64,
  189
Kennedy, Joseph, 140
Kennedy, Robert F., 55, 58–60,
  62, 64, 179, 180
Kent, James, 13–14, 176
Kerr, Aubrey, 43, 58
Kerr, Robert S., 43, 44, 48,
  54–65, 90, 139–41, 178–80,
  193
Kerr-McGee Corporation, 44,
  90
Keyes v. School District No. 1,
  105, 188
King, Martin Luther, Jr., 85,
  111, 184
Klein, Gerald B. ("K. G."),
  57–58, 61, 63, 179
Kovaleff, Theodore, 173
Krebs, Ernest T., Sr., 147
Ku Klux Klan, 48, 100, 178, 190

Laetrile, 9, 146–56, 194
Lake Stanley Draper (Okla.), 54

Langley, Edwin, 124–25
Langston University, 79
Laurents, Arthur, 16
Lawson, Wayne, 124
Lee, Josh, 38, 40, 41, 43, 63
Lewis, Anthony, 64, 179, 180
Lewis, David T., 142
Lincoln University, 79
Luper, Clara, 84–85, 87, 104,
  136–37, 185, 186, 188, 192–93
Lutz, Raymond P., 97

McAlester prison, 120–24,
  128–31, 134; riot at, 124–26.
  See also Oklahoma prison
  system
McCarthy, Eugene, 59, 179
McCarthy, Sheryl, 137
McCarty, J. D., 61, 65–68,
  180–81
McClellan, George, 139
McClelland, Bruce, 63–64
McCracken, Leo, 124
McCree, Wade, 153
McKay, Monroe, 135
McLaurin, George, 80
McLaurin v. Oklahoma State
  Board of Regents, 80, 183–84
Madison, James, 13
Marland, E. W., 40, 41, 178
Marshall, Chief Justice John,
  14, 143, 174
Marshall, Ronald C., 134
Meacham, Larry, 68
Mellott, Arthur J., 7
Missouri ex rel. Gaines v.
  Canada, 79, 80
Monnet, Julien C., 29–34, 68,
  137, 157, 177, 181, 185
Monroney, A. S. ("Mike"),
  47–48, 50, 142, 175
Moon, E. C., 89

Moon, F. D., 82
Morgan, Anne Hodges, 62, 140, 179, 180, 193
Murrah, A. P., 36–38, 57, 63; appointment as judge, 41, 57; and desegregation, 88, 95–96, 187; and judicial elections, 38
Murray, Johnston, 81–82
Murray, William H. ("Alfalfa Bill"), 77, 82, 182–83
Myrdal, Gunnar, 75

National Association for the Advancement of Colored People (NAACP), 3, 7, 72, 78–81, 84–87, 89, 94–95, 101, 190; NAACP Legal Defense Fund (LDF), 72, 78, 108, 111, 113, 114, 116, 181–82, 187, 189
National Conference of Christians and Jews, 69
National Education Association, 111
Nigh, George, 133, 135–36
Nixon, Richard M., 55, 57, 58

Oklahoma A&M College (Oklahoma State University), 79
Oklahoma City University, 69
Oklahoma Constitutional Convention, 74–75, 77, 182; and segregation, 74–75, 182–83
Oklahoma Department of Corrections, 121, 124, 127, 128, 134
Oklahoma National Guard, 9, 26–27, 118, 155
Oklahoma prison system, 9, 68, 120, 127–31, 133, 135–36
Oklahoma Supreme Court, 51–53, 69–70; corruption on, 50–53

Opala, Marian, 69, 181
Otoe & Missouria v. United States, 44–50, 178
Owen, Ben, 33
Owen, Robert L., 40

Parker, W. B., 112
Parks, Thelma, 110
Payne v. Tennessee, 5–6
Pearson, Drew, 139
Peltason, Jack, 83, 185
Phillips, Leon ("Red"), 41, 178
Pipestem, Francis, 47
Pleasant Hill school district, 86, 186
Plessy v. Ferguson, 4, 81
Porter, E. Melvin, 87
Posey, Barbara, 85
Prison Overcrowding Emergency Act, 136
Prison reform, 9, 120–36, 191–92

Rayburn, Sam, 56
Rehnquist, Chief Justice William, 5, 108–109
Roerson, Henry, 100
Roe v. Wade, 3, 156, 193, 195
Roosevelt, Franklin D., 41, 178
Roosevelt, Theodore, 74
Rutherford v. United States, 146–56, 194–95
Rutherford, Glen L., 147–49, 154, 156

Savage, Royce, 38, 43, 63
Schlesinger, Arthur, 64, 179–80
Schneider, Phyllis S., 147
Scott, Lederle J., 87
Seay, Frank, 135
Seigenthaler, John, 60–61, 180

Selected Investments v. *Oklahoma Tax Commission*. See *Tyree* v. *Selected Investments Corporation*
Shields, Susanna, 196
Shunatona, Baptiste ("Bat"), 45, 46, 49
Sipuel, Ada Lois. *See* Fisher, Ada Lois Sipuel
Sipuel v. *Board of Regents*, 79–80, 174, 183–84
Smith, William French, 119–20
Sorenson, Theodore, 140, 193
Souter, Justice David, 108
Stare decisis, 5–6, 156
Starr, Kenneth, 110
Steller, Arthur, 114
Stevens, Justice John Paul, 109
Stewart, James E., 78, 115, 190
Stowe, Juanita, 147
Summers, Hardy, 70, 181
Swann v. *Charlotte-Mecklenburg Board of Education*, 98, 105, 106, 111, 118
Swatek, Matthew Anton, 38

Tate, U. Simpson, 87
Thomas, John William Elmer, 48, 140–41
Thomas, Justice Clarence, 137, 156, 176, 193
Troy, Frosty, 64–65, 67, 70, 75, 180, 181, 183, 191

Truman, Harry, 49
Tyree v. *Selected Investments Corporation*, 50–53, 116

Ungerman, Irvine, 124, 127
U.S. v. *Texas*, 139, 193
University of California Medical School, 147
University of Missouri, 79
University of Oklahoma, 29, 33, 34, 79–80, 97
Urban League of Oklahoma City, 79, 83, 183

Walker, John, 95
Wallace, William, 57
Waring, J. Waties, 4
Warren, Chief Justice Earl, 48, 80–81, 158–59, 184
Washington, James M., 174
Watkins, T. H., 46, 178
Watts, Wade, 101
Webb, James E., 90
Wheat, Willis, 92–95
White, Justice Byron ("Whizzer"), 58–59, 61–62, 95
Willis, Bill, 132–33
Woodmansee, T. J., 34
Worcester v. *Georgia*, 5, 143, 174, 194

Yeazell, Stephen, 118, 190, 191
Young, John, 129
Young, William, 15, 176

	DATE DUE		

R0123007437   SSCCA   S
                        B
                        B676W

HOUSTON PUBLIC LIBRARY
CENTRAL LIBRARY

5/6/94